TEACHING AND LEARNING STRATEGIES IN PHYSICAL EDUCATION

A Report from the BAALPE
National Study Group

BAALPE

*British Association of Advisers and Lecturers
in Physical Education*

Teaching and Learning Strategies in Physical Education

Copyright © The British Association of Advisers and Lecturers in Physical Education 1989

ISBN 1 871228 02 6

First published 1989 by **The British Association of Advisers and Lecturers in Physical Education**

Designed, produced and distributed on behalf of BAALPE by **White Line Press**, 60 Bradford Road, Stanningley, Leeds LS28 6EF

All orders to be sent to White Line Press

Printed in Great Britain
at the Alden Press, Oxford

TEACHING AND LEARNING
STRATEGIES IN
PHYSICAL EDUCATION

01

CONTENTS

PART I: INTRODUCTION

PART II: CASE STUDIES

PART III: OUTCOME

APPENDIX

PART I

INTRODUCTION

he review of teaching strategy
nd style proved to be a cross-
urricular involvement. The project
roved invaluable, not only to the
eaching approach in PE, but also
for other subject disciplines,
thanks to the improvement of non-
specialists."

"The project has made me more
aware of teaching approaches and
the importance of these to the
learning process."

"No one strategy can be used in
isolation. A balanced mixture of
several strategies is more likely to
cater for all pupils' needs."

"As a department we felt that we
were very didactic in our
approach. We did use other styles
of teaching, but were not totally
aware of this at the time."

BAALPE.
National
Study Group

1.1 National Study Group on Teaching and Learning Strategies in Physical Education

In 1986 local education authorities
were invited to participate in a national study group investigating different
approaches used in the teaching and
learning of physical education.

Ten authorities agreed to participate,
and throughout the school year
1986–87 they addressed themselves
to the main aims of the project, which
were:

● to promote a greater awareness
among PE teachers of the range of
strategies and styles that they
might employ in their teaching;

● to monitor the process of exploring
different strategies or a selected
style of teaching;

● to attempt to evaluate the effective-
ness of such teaching, both for the
teacher and for the pupils.

Each participating LEA agreed to
support two or three teachers as they
explored the use of different selected
strategies or a particular style.

> **Teaching strategy**: a particular
> tactic or technique chosen for
> some specific occasion.
>
> **Teaching style**: the general pat-
> tern created by using a particular
> set of strategies.

Mosston's continuum of styles was
used to provide the basic framework
(see page 12).

Meetings were held within each LEA
to consider each team's particular
contribution to the project, and how
this in turn would support staff development and curriculum review
within the particular school or
authority.

From September 1986 to July 1987,
LEAs each pursued their own area of
study, focusing on their selected
strategies or style of teaching. Each
teacher undertook to identify a particular unit of work with a particular
group, and to record, monitor and
evaluate all aspects of this unit of
work. The results were then published
within each LEA, and subsequently
among the other participants in the
project; a selection of these case
studies appear in this book.

2. TEACHING STRATEGIES AND STYLES

The setting-up of the National Study Group on Teaching and Learning Strategies in Physical Education coincided with several other developments:

● the circulation of *The Curriculum 5–16* (DES 1985);

● the implementation of GCSE;

● the development of TVEI from the pilot stage.

A common emphasis is to be found in all these publications and initiatives. All of them focus on *process*:

● active learning with increasing elements of negotiation;

● shared responsibility for teaching and learning between teachers and pupils;

● greater interaction, both between pupils and teachers and within each group.

Participation in the study group gave teachers the opportunity to explore different approaches to learning and teaching with outside support. They were thus in a position to respond with confidence to national initiatives.

2.1 Learning and Teaching Approaches

"The influence of learning activities and teaching styles on what is learned and how well it is learned has already been noted. The more the curriculum includes objectives which go beyond subject matter and promote the development of particular attitudes and capabilities, the stronger are the implications for the variety and range of teaching approaches to be employed if all the objectives are to be achieved. As far as possible, teaching should match the abilities, attainments, interests and experiences of pupils; in addition to factual knowledge, it is important to develop concepts, skills and attitudes, and pupils should learn in a variety of ways according to the task in hand. It follows that no single style of teaching will be suitable for all purposes: sometimes it will be appropriate to teach the class as a whole; sometimes pupils should carry considerable responsibility for deciding the direction of their work."

"Active learning, and a sense of purpose and success, enhance pupils' enjoyment, interest, confidence and sense of personal worth; passive learning and inappropriate styles can lead to frustration and failure."

The Curriculum 5–16 (DES.1985)

"My selection and use of strategies has become a conscious and informed choice based on my perception of the needs of the group."

"The class size (34–36) did present many problems. In small-group situations it took a long time to go from group to group and pose questions. It was difficult to offer appropriate help on a large scale."

"The girls became very articulate in their responses, but they could not convert the theory into practice owing to their physical limitations."

"I found reciprocal teaching had much to offer the pupils' social development. Even the shy lad found he had something to say to his partner."

Many PE teachers already use a range of teaching styles and a variety of strategies within their normal good practice. However, clarifying these approaches in order to raise teachers' awareness can only be beneficial. This was achieved in the project by using the framework, or spectrum, proposed by Mosston in *From Command to Discovery* (1981).

It should, however, be stressed that it was not the purpose of the project to view the framework as a rigid, systematic procedure in which a teacher works in one or other style throughout his or her teaching. The point of the framework was to provide a clear base from which to begin to analyse the process of teaching. If a teacher wishes to widen the range of teaching strategies used in order to facilitate different kinds of learning amongst his or her pupils, it is necessary to analyse the processes of both teaching and learning.

Mosston bases his spectrum of teaching styles on the following assertions:

1. Teaching is a process of *decision-making* in which both teachers and pupils are involved to a greater or lesser extent.

2. All teachers can consciously learn and use techniques which allow for more (or less) decision-making behaviour on the part of their pupils (ie they learn to become independent).

3. Analysis of teaching behaviour is hindered by considering the process as being invariably *either* one style *or* another (eg either command or discovery). Teaching behaviour forms a continuum, and a good teacher should be able to apply the styles appropriate to the desired outcomes.

4. Teach*ing* behaviour is independent of teach*er* behaviour (in which personality is a prime factor). All personalities within the teaching profession can still have access to the whole range of teaching styles and strategies.

To simplify a complex process, Mosston suggests that there are three main stages of decision-making involved in the teaching process. These are:

● *pre-impact decisions* — ie planning;

● *impact decisions* — ie the actual teaching/learning experience;

● *post-impact decisions* — ie feedback and evaluation.

Pre-impact decisions are concerned with such things as objectives, subject matter, time, organisation, presentation. Such decisions are all made prior to the teaching episode itself.

Impact decisions are those adjustments which are made during the performance of a task or lesson.

Post-impact decisions include decisions concerning the evaluation of the performance and feedback from the learner to the teacher.

Together these stages form the anatomy of a teaching style, and are implicitly or explicitly part of every teaching episode. An episode is a unit of time spent in a particular style.

A lesson may be made up of many episodes (ie a number of styles may be apparent in a single lesson).

Figure 2.1 gives a brief resumé of the teaching styles, outlining the essential characteristics of each style and the most likely objectives of a teacher who selects that style. The link between different objectives and the appropriate choice of teaching style then becomes clearer.

Figure 2.1 Styles of Teaching

Style	Essential characteristics	Likely objectives	Focus
A. Command	● All decisions made by the teacher. ● Learners do as they are told. ● The class responds as a group.	● Conformity to a single standard of performance. ● Efficiency in the use of time to acquire skills. ● Safety and discipline.	Motor development
B. Practice	● Most decisions made by the teacher. ● The learner makes some decisions at the impact stage. ● A period of practice time on a task is set by the teacher, who can help individuals.	● To improve skill. ● To make learners aware of the relationship between commitment of time and quality of product or outcome. ● To help learners to judge their level of performance.	Motor development
C. Reciprocal	● Planned by teacher, executed by learners. ● Learners work in pairs, one taking role of teacher and other of learner; roles are exchanged. ● Clear criteria, generally on cards, are an integral part of this style. ● The teacher gives responsibility for execution to pupils; works through pupil-teacher.	● To engage pupils in social situations. ● To develop communication skills. ● To develop skills of observing, listening and analysing. ● To heighten awareness of others, patience and tolerance. ● To provide for maximum feedback from each performer.	Social (and motor) development
D. Self-check	● Planned by teacher. Performance criteria essential. ● Individuals check their own performance, ie make decisions at the impact stage. ● Post-impact decisions made in relation to clearly stated criteria.	● To help learners assess their own performance. ● To help personal development in terms of honesty and the ability to be objective. ● To help learners recognise their own limitations.	Personal (and motor) development
E. Inclusion	● Planned by teacher. ● Individuals check their own performance, starting at their own levels and progressing appropriately. ● Tasks are set so that individual progress is highlighted.	● To maximise involvement at appropriate levels of performance. ● To accommodate individual differences. ● To help learners rationalise their aspirations with reality. ● To enable everyone to succeed. Personal (and motor) development	

All the above styles display teacher control at pre-impact stage

Style	Essential characteristics	Likely objectives	Focus
F. Guided discovery	● The teacher plans a target and systematically leads the learners to discover the target. ● Questioning by the teacher is fundamental to this style. ● The choice of the appropriate steps in the discovery process is critical to success. ● Redirection of learners who go off at a tangent.	● To engage learners in a convergent process of discovery. ● To develop sequential discovery skills and consequences of action. ● To develop patience while progressing through skilful matching of response to questions and stimuli.	Cognitive (and motor) development

Figure 2.1 (continued)

Style	Essential characteristics	Likely objectives	Focus
G. Problem-solving (divergent)	● The teacher presents questions or a problem situation, and pupils are invited to discover an alternative solution. ● Frequently pupils are organised into groups to encourage shared thinking. ● Pupils contribute to decisions at all stages, since their response may determine the next move.	● To develop the ability to work on problems and solve them. ● To develop insights into the structure of an activity through the search for a solution. ● To develop the ability to verify solutions. ● To encourage independent thinking. ● To promote learners' confidence in their own ideas and responses.	Cognitive and social (plus motor and personal) development
H. Individual programme	● The learner plans and designs the programme. ● The teacher proposes the subject matter and approves the programme.	● To encourage independent planning and assessment under guidance. ● To reveal the level of understanding through application. ● To encourage persistence in completing a programme. ● To promote self-confidence.	Cognitive and personal (plus motor) development
I. Learner initiatives	● The learner selects the content, and plans and designs the programme with the approval of the teacher. ● The learner executes the programme and submits an evaluation to the teacher.	● To encourage and develop independence. ● To display understanding through selection and application. ● To encourage the acceptance of personal responsibility. ● To develop self-confidence.	Cognitive and personal (plus motor) development
J. Self-teaching	The learner is both teacher and learner, working fully independently.		Cognitive, personal and motor development

The analytical spectrum of teaching styles is based on the varying nature of the contract between the teacher and the learner. Teaching is thus seen as a continuous series of relationships evolving between teacher and learner, which can be critically considered. Understanding the teaching process in terms of deliberately transferring responsibility for making decisions is a significant aspect in the current climate with its increased emphasis on the learner becoming more responsible for, and involved in, the learning process.

The ability to move deliberately along the continuum proposed by Mosston is not only effective in meeting the learner's needs as selected by the teacher's objectives, but also increases a teacher's competence and status. Now that accountability and self-appraisal are being sought, these are necessary professional skills, and it is important that teachers should be able to analyse their own teaching clearly and objectively.

The teacher should be able to use both a range of styles and a variety of strategies which may contribute to different styles. These should be selected and applied in relation to pupil need and to the particular outcome desired by the teacher. Several styles and many strategies may feature in a single lesson when the teacher is sufficiently confident and experienced.

> "Good teachers need a variety of approaches and patterns of working, and the flexibility to call on several different strategies within the space of one lesson."
>
> [DES 1985]

Figure 2.2 Promoting Good Practice in the Teaching of Physical Education

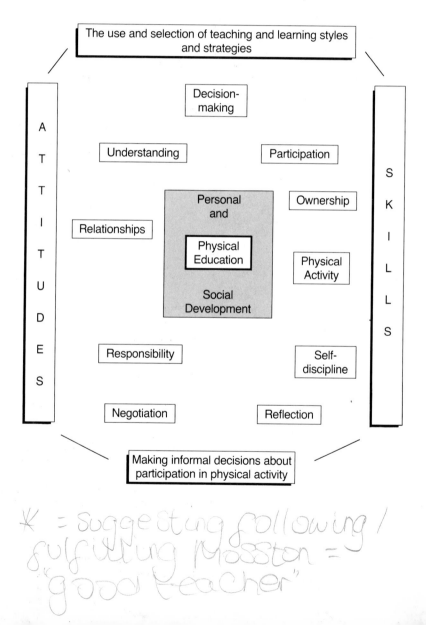

3. DETAILS OF THE PROJECT

3.1 The Participants and the Styles Explored

Each of the teachers participating in the project selected a particular focus for further investigation as his or her contribution. This focus was generally on one teaching style, but in some cases was on selected strategies which were felt to be essential to a style. Teachers in Somerset, for example, analysed key strategies that go to make up style G.

Having identified the focus, each teacher then worked with a group in a particular unit of work. Units of work varied in length according to the school and its curriculum, but they were generally between five and six weeks.

These units of work are summarised below, categorised according to the teaching style which provided the focus. Each unit was written up in considerable detail, and anyone wishing to have further information should contact the LEA concerned.

This summary is followed by a series of case studies, selected by teachers on the project. They were chosen on the basis that they provided very useful information and insights which should be shared with as many people as possible.

The justification for limiting the focus to one or two styles, or to selected strategies, relates to the point of clarification made earlier. A single focus helps the teacher identify differences clearly, then to explore specific techniques in order to develop a range of skills and relate these to desired outcomes (objectives). The discipline of working within one style in fact forces the teacher to clarify his or her techniques in relation to the desired outcomes. As teachers become more confident and more experienced, so they can be expected to demonstrate an awareness of a range of teaching approaches and the ability to select the appropriate one for a particular learning outcome.

Figure 3.1 Participants in the Project

LEA	Activity and Style	Age/Gender	School	Teacher(s)
Barnet	1. Gymnastics C. Reciprocal	11–13/mixed	Ashmole School	S Holland M Peplow K Henderson
	2. Gymnastics C. Reciprocal	12–13/mixed	Bishop Douglass School	B Wilson
Dudley	1. Dance/Movement C. Reciprocal	7–12/mixed (hearing impaired)	Ashwood Park Primary School	Ruth McShane
	2. Dance/Movement C. Reciprocal	10–11/mixed		
	3. Basketball (joint project) C. Reciprocal	12–13/girls 12–13/mixed	High Park School The Coseley School	Julie Dignon Roy Anderson Ian Spode (Advisory Teacher)
Norfolk	1. Invasion games (for cross-phase development) G. Problem-solving	12–13/boys	Dereham Northgate High School	Chris Price
	2. Soccer G. Problem-solving 3. Games-making G. Problem-solving	11–12/mixed	King Edward VII High School, Kings Lynn	P Tebay
	4. Games (netball, hockey, tennis) G. Problem-solving	11–12/girls	Downham Market High School	Elizabeth Tyler
Redbridge	1. Netball C. Reciprocal	11–12/girls	Trinity RC High School	Leslie Hindmarsh
	2. Gymnastics C. Reciprocal G. Problem-solving	11–12/girls 12–13/girls	Mayfield High School	Judith Rock
Rotherham	1. Gymnastics C. Reciprocal	12–13/girls	Kimberworth Comprehensive School	Ivy Dorchester Heather Mile R Garnshaw
	2. Cricket C. Reciprocal	11–13/boys		
	3. Gymnastics (sports acrobatics) C. Reciprocal	12–13/girls	Thrybergh Comprehensive School	Mavis Taylor

Figure 3.1 (continued)

LEA	Activity and Style	Age/Gender	School	Teacher(s)
Rotheram (continued)	4. Racket skills F. Guided discovery C. Reciprocal	11–12/mixed	Wath Comprehensive School	Pat Mitchell C Cox
	5. Athletics C. Reciprocal			Pat Mitchell G Brammer
	6. Gymnastics E. Inclusion	11–12/boys	Aston Comprehensive School	R Selkirk
	7. Swimming E. Inclusion	11–12/boys	Kimberworth Comprehensive School	John Gray
Somerset	1. Net games (key factors of listening, decision-making, reflecting)	11–12/girls	Crispin School, Street	Ann-Marie Latham
	2. Invasion games (key factors as above)	11–12/mixed	King Alfred's School, Burnham-on-Sea	Paul Stoddart
	3. Creative games G. Problem-solving	primary/mixed	St Andrew's Junior School, Burnham-on-Sea	Debra Wilcox
Sunderland	1. Swimming, athletics, gymnastics C. Reciprocal	11–13/mixed	Hylton Red House School	J Young
	2. "Now get out of that" G. Problem-solving	14–15/mixed	Biddick School, Washington	J Sturrock
Surrey	1. Volleyball C. Reciprocal	13–14/mixed	Bishop David Brown School	Alison Vinai
	2. Gymnastics C. Reciprocal G. Problem-solving	11–12/mixed	South Farnham Middle School	Sylvia Mundy
	3. Gymnastics (analysis of teachers' use of styles)	12–13/mixed	Therfield Secondary School	Olia Inak
Walsall	1. Gymnastics C. Reciprocal	11–12/boys	T P Riley Community School	D Gott
	2. Dance F. Guided discovery	11–12/girls	Alumwell Community School	Jackie Callicott
	3. Games G. Problem-solving	10–11/mixed	Leamore JMI School	Sue Orton

> "It is interesting to note after the completion of the project that this style of teaching has had a positive influence on all the teachers. It has made us more aware of the personal and social needs of the pupils, and we are all consciously adjusting our styles of teaching to accommodate to these needs."

> "It is an ongoing process which, once initiated, can be slowly built upon, encouraging more trust between teacher and pupils and, indeed, pupil and pupil."

PART II

CASE STUDIES

> "Reciprocal teaching necessarily involved pupils in the cognitive skills of reading, interpreting, communicating, observing, analysing, evaluating and modifying the responses of their partners."

> "It is essential for the task-sheets/work-cards to have a language which is readily accessible to pupils of all ability levels."

> "I found reciprocal teaching a useful strategy for refining the psychomotor skills for set tasks which can be reproduced on task-cards."

> "It took a long time to get through the work."

4.1 Case Study 1

T P Riley Community School, Walsall
Class: 1st-year Gymnastics
Theme: Reciprocal Teaching
Teacher: D Gott

Aim

To explore reciprocal teaching as a strategy for teaching the theme of locomotion in gymnastics.

The teaching group was a mixed-ability class of 26 eleven-year-old boys in the first term of their first year at secondary school. Individual children came from any one of five cluster schools. Previous knowledge and experience of gymnastics within the class was diverse.

My project covered six weekly lessons, each lasting an hour (including the time required for changing and showering). In addition I used a one-hour preliminary lesson in order to familiarise myself with some of the less familiar strategies outlined in Mosston's text.

A detailed diary of the six-week project is given on pages 23–29. Information is recorded under the following headings:

- work covered;
- strategy used;
- questions and responses;
- outcomes.

I found the preliminary session most useful. It enabled me to place reciprocal teaching into context with my tried-and-tested battery of strategies — and my less tried-and-tested strategies. The results helped shape my project, and provoked several thoughts regarding the uses of different teaching strategies:

1. It caused me to examine and identify my existing teaching strategies.

2. It confirmed my assumption that it would be difficult (and false) to isolate and use one strategy only in a lesson or series of lessons. Thus within my project I used a number of strategies (identified within the diary), but highlighted reciprocal teaching wherever and whenever I thought this strategy could be used.

3. My selection of strategies became a conscious and informed choice based on my perception of the needs of the group.

The Effects of Reciprocal Teaching

The development of understanding and creativity

Reciprocal teaching necessarily involved pupil-teachers in the cognitive skills of reading, interpreting, communicating, observing, analysing, evaluating and modifying the responses of their partners. Both pupils and pupil-teachers, therefore, were actively engaged in their own learning and in the teaching of others. To teach others properly requires reasonably developed cognitive skills, an understanding of what the task is about, and a training or natural flair for communicating these ideas to others.

A number of pragmatic problems were raised during the six-week project, which I feel are issues central to the strategy:

1. In my mixed-ability class, some pupils had reading difficulties. It is essential for the task-sheets/work-cards to have a language which is readily accessible to pupils of all ability levels.

2. The work-card/task-sheet diagrams need to be well laid out, explicit and easy to understand — almost professionally done.

3. We must initially be prepared to supplement reciprocal teaching with alternative strategies in order to develop a critical eye for observation and attention to detail, and to promote the general concept of quality. (I personally used guided discovery and teacher-directed strategies — see diary.)

Nevertheless, in spite of these limitations, the strategy provided opportunity for pupils to exercise and develop their cognitive skills, and improvement was evident as the project progressed.

I found it interesting to note that in general those pupils who first acted as teachers and then as performers acquired the skills more quickly than their partners. Some latent learning during the teaching process may possibly explain this.

I found that creativity within reciprocal teaching was very inhibiting for both pupil-teacher and performer. The pupil-teacher was generally much happier and more confident when the task was a single specific movement. The task-card itself was more simple and more explicit than an educational gymnastics sequence involving three or four different movements. The pupil-teacher's confidence and security (or lack of it) was conveyed to the performer, who then reflected this in the quality of his movement.

After a period of time, when both pupils and pupil-teachers have built up a sufficient vocabulary of movement (through reciprocal teaching or otherwise), perhaps reciprocal teaching could be an effective strategy for developing quality from a creative theme.

Improvement was evident, however, as the project progressed, and pupils did gain from sharing their ideas.

Social development

I found reciprocal teaching had much to offer the pupils' social development. The notion of communicating a series of tasks, prompted by a task-card, to a partner who responds through movement, was thought to be very exciting and fun to do (though note earlier criticisms). Even the shy lad found he had something to say to his partner. As the project progressed, confidence and enthusiasm grew, and the change-over of partners ensured social integration. (I wonder how a mixed-sex group would have responded.)

The development of psychomotor skills

I found reciprocal teaching a useful strategy for refining the psychomotor skills for set tasks which can be reproduced on task-cards. I would also make the following observations:

1. Although pupil-teacher and pupil are involved in their own learning, the whole process takes much longer than a more teacher-directed strategy. This will necessarily affect timing, and allowances will have to be made for this in curriculum planning.

2. If the task-cards are well produced, they are an aid for the (weaker) class teacher of gymnastics as well as for the pupil-teacher.

3. A task-card system may enhance progress evaluation and profiling in some areas of gymnastics.

Figure 4.1 Locomotion: Lesson 1

17 September 1986

Strategy	Work covered	Questions and responses	Outcomes
Experiential and guided discovery Teacher-directed	Warm-up and introduction to initial basic rules/safety when working in a gym.	1. "Move around the gym in any direction you like." 2. **"Stop!"**: an explanation of what the command means; safety implications; use of alternative words of similar meaning to extend vocabulary.	1. Pupils (not unexpectedly) charged around, lapping the gym, giving no real thought to what they were doing or how they were doing it. 2. Pupils came to understand the basic rules of working in the gymnasium — also the need to listen and respond through movement, and to interpret the meaning of different words.
Questions and answers Guided discovery Problem-solving Individual learning	Locomotion Basic movement Introduction	3. How to run quietly: "on your toes; lips closed; don't bump into anyone; eyes open; think; don't go too fast." 4. How to make moving around the gym into a more interesting activity, both for the performer and for the spectator: changes in direction, speed, step patterns and height levels. 5. Taking one aspect at a time: moving around the gym and changing direction, say, every 7–10 paces. 6. Each change of direction accompanied by a change of speed. What is meant by a change of speed? (Standing still, stationary movement, walking, slow and fast running.) 7. "What connection can you make between how fast you are travelling and the angle of turn?" (The slower you go, the more you can vary the angle of turn.)	3. Pupils responded to more direction; their answers to the problem led to greater understanding, awareness and control. 4. Pupils started to think, analyse and work out a series of possibilities. 5. The concept was generally understood when travelling forwards. But further possibilities needed to be explored, such as moving sideways or backwards, and incorporating changes in direction. 6. Examining the concept of speed, and analysing the various possibilities, led to a greater understanding of movement. 7. Pupils showed an awareness of body control, changes in speed, changes in direction.

Figure 4.1 (continued)

Strategy	Work covered	Questions and responses	Outcomes
As previously stated	As previously stated	8. "What is meant by step patterns?" (Hopping, running, skipping, jumping etc.)	8. Pupils examined the concept of step patterns and the range of possibilities.
		9. "Try three or four different types."	9. Pupils experimented, experienced, analysed and selected from a range of possibilities.
Experiential problem-solving Guided discovery	Linking a movement sequence	10. A **sequence**, showing three changes of direction, three changes of speed and three changes of stepping pattern.	10. Definitions of the term *sequence*. Experience in linking movements together fluently with a start and finish. Pupils were a little lost, and not sure of expectations or quality.
Teacher-directed Questions and answers	Observation	11. Examples highlighted. Individual work.	11. Refinement of movement; critical observation of movement; quality of movement; good start and finish.
Reciprocal teaching		12. "Can you help your partner to improve his or her sequence? Think about a good start, a good finish, poise, control and quality." Pupils used the worksheet entitled *helpful hints*. 13. Pupils in the teacher role were asked how they thought their performer was getting on. How might they get him to improve? What should they be telling him?	12. Pupils engaged actively in their own learning and in the teaching of others. In spite of the *helpful hints*, the quality of the teaching and refinement of movement was limited, no doubt because the pupils lacked knowledge and experience, were short of movement vocabulary and used little movement analysis. Nevertheless, social contact was highlighted and some improvements in motor skills were evident.

Figure 4.2 Locomotion: Lesson 2

24 September 1986

Strategy	Work covered	Questions and responses	Outcomes
Experiential and guided discovery	Warm-up and recap of previous week's work.	1. "Move around the gym in any direction you like."	1. Pupils showed more awareness of space and of each other; most pupils changed direction; some continued to lap the gym; some showed changes in step patterns.
Teacher-directed		2. **"Stop!"**	2. All pupils responded positively and alertly to the command **"Stop!"**
Question and answer	Recap of previous week: moving around the gym.	3. How to run quietly.	3. Pupils remembered the answers and responded appropriately through movement.
Question and answer		4. How to make movements more interesting.	4. Pupils remembered the previous week's sequence.
Guided (re)discovery	A sequence	5. The previous week's sequence.	5. Memory through performance.
Teacher-directed	Observation	6. Examples highlighted and movements refined. "How do you think [so and so] can improve his sequence?"	6. Observation, analysis and refinement of other pupils' movements made pupils aware of the need to pay attention to both quality detail (starts, finishes, poise, control, flow).
Question and answer Experiential Same direction	Experimenting with movement, using range of levels.	7. "What else can be done to make the movements different?" Changes in levels/height, exploring the different possibilities.	7. Pupils started thinking, experimenting, working out a range of possibilities: off the floor (jumps of various types); upright; crouched; squat; on the floor.
Experiential and guided discovery	Sequence formation Problem-solving	8. Creating a sequence: four directions, four levels.	8. Pupils experimented within a range of movement; some demonstrated changes in speed and stepping patterns in addition to the task set (this was noted).
Reciprocal teaching	Refinement of skills	9. "Can you help your partner to improve his sequence?" Pupils used the *helpful hints* sheet. 10. Pupil-teachers were asked in turn how they were progressing etc (see Lesson 1, item 13).	9. Pupils were actively engaged in their own learning, and in observing, analysing, teaching and refining the movements of other pupils. The social benefits were self-evident, together with an increasing awareness of body control and quality and of the need to achieve them. There was more limited awareness of how to help others to develop this. The *helpful hints* sheet, along with imitation of any teacher-directed parts of the lesson, provided some guidelines that were exploited by the more astute pupils.

Figure 4.3 Locomotion: Lesson 3

1 October 1986

Strategy	Work covered	Questions and responses	Outcomes
Experiential and guided discovery	Warm-up: recap of previous week's work.	1. "Move around the gym in any direction you like."	1. Most pupils were beginning to show an awareness of space, of each other and of changes in direction, level, steps etc.
Teacher-directed		2. "**Stop!**"	2. A positive and alert response to command safety procedures.
Guided (re)discovery Question and answer Guided discovery	Use of large and small body parts to take weight while travelling	3. Recap of previous week's work, including sequences and levels. 4. Movements using large and small body parts, and their relationship to different movement levels.	3. Pupils remembered and responded through movement. 4. Pupils experimented and discovered different ways of using body parts: that movements using large body parts operate only at ground level, while those using small body parts can operate at all levels.
Experiential problem-solving	Incorporating body parts into a sequence	5. Creating a small single-direction sequence showing a change from small to large body parts and back to small body parts.	5. Pupils experimented and discovered a range of possibilities, all involving some form of rolling movement.
Teacher-directed Question and answer	Observation	6. Examples highlighted and movements refined. "How do you think [so and so] can improve his performance?"	6. Pupils became very critical of sloppy, uncontrolled movement. They made good starts and finishes and paid attention to detail. They were learning to be critical and aware of the need for quality.
Reciprocal teaching	A set movement: prone fall — sideways body roll — return to standing position.	7. "How can you help your partner to perform the roll described in your worksheets?" (These included diagrams and *helpful hints*.)	7. Pupils engaged actively in their own learning, and in the reading, understanding and communication of a specific movement to their partners. Pupils found teaching a specific movement difficult. Some pupils had difficulty in reading and/or understanding what was required. Worksheets must therefore be in language that is readily accessible to pupils of all ability levels. Pupils who performed second generally acquired the skill quicker than their partners, no doubt because of latent learning during the teaching process.
Reciprocal teaching	Placing movements into a set sequence	8. "Help your partner to perform the following sequence: start — run — jump — prone fall — sideways body roll — return to feet — finish."	8. Pupils found this more difficult, though they were becoming more critically aware of body control, body shape and alignment.

Figure 4.4 Locomotion: Lesson 4

8 October 1986

Strategy	Work covered	Questions and responses	Outcomes
Experiential and guided discovery Teacher-directed	Warm-up: recap of previous week's work.	1. "Move around the gym in any direction you like." 2. "**Stop!**": reference made to need for this command.	1/2. A more pleasing response from pupils, with a variety of movements, directions, step patterns etc. An obvious awareness of space and control, although the movement quality was of a lower standard here than when practised in the main part of the lesson (this was noted).
Reciprocal teaching Reciprocal teaching	Previous week's set movement and set sequence	3. Recap of previous week's work, using the same work-sheet. 4 Practising the previous week's set sequence.	3/4. Pupils showed obvious enjoyment and enthusiasm with this strategy. Pupils of all ability levels (even the non-doers) were experiencing levels of success in teaching others how to perform a set task.
Reciprocal teaching	Gymnastics movement: forward roll	5. "Can you help your partner to perform the task on the worksheet?" (This was read through with the group, carefully identifying and explaining each phase.)	5. The pupils reacted with enthusiasm and enjoyment, for a number of possible reasons: ● they were becoming familiar with the technique; ● both teacher and performer experienced success; ● the set task was a specific movement, illustrated in readily identifiable teaching phases; ● the class teacher went through the sheet first with all the pupils. However, pupils with reading difficulties continued to present problems.

Figure 4.5 Locomotion: Lesson 5

15 October 1986

Strategy	Work covered	Questions and responses	Outcomes
Experiential and guided discovery Teacher-directed	Warm-up: recap of previous week's work.	1. "Move around the gym in any direction you like." 2. **"Stop!"**	1/2. Pupils demonstrated an increasing awareness of space, direction and different ways of moving. Some informal (and unprompted) competition was starting to develop among certain pupils as they experimented with a range of possibilities.
Teacher-directed		3. Examples highlighted with reference to points of quality.	3. Pupils were developing a critical eye for movement and paying more attention to detail.
Reciprocal teaching	Recap of previous week's work: forward roll.	4. "Can you help your partner to perform the task on the worksheet? Make sure you have a different partner this week." (The latter request was met initially with some dismay.)	4. The change of partner encouraged better social mixing. Recapping the previous week's work gave new partnerships some sense of continuity, security and confidence of expectations. Pupils worked enthusiastically and confidently in spite of new partner groupings, and most were able to remember the range of movement and fine points of detail.
Reciprocal teaching	A set sequence, incorporating a forward roll into the sequence first practised in Lessons 3 and 4.	5. "Help your partner perform the following sequence: starting position — travel — jump — forward roll — finishing position." (Details given on worksheets together with *helpful hints*.)	5. Pupils felt less secure when teaching, modifying and refining movements across a sequence, even though the sequence had already been practised in an earlier lesson. This may possibly have been due to the apparent vagueness of individual sequences compared with the explicitness of a single gymnastic movement. This was to be tested further in the next lesson. Nevertheless, the pupils were communicating, their social development was enhanced, and there was evidence of psychomotor improvement.
Experiential Guided discovery Teacher-directed	Balancing.	6. "Demonstrate balancing on three parts of the body, noting large and small body parts used, alignment, shape, symmetry and asymmetry."	6. Pupils explored a range of possibilities, and analysed and selected appropriate balances. They reacted positively to direction and refinement of skill. Pupils were asked to explore the possibilities of linking the forward roll with balances for the following lesson.

Figure 4.6 Locomotion: Lesson 6

22 October 1986

Strategy	Work covered	Questions and responses	Outcomes
Experiential guided discovery Teacher-directed	Warm-up: recap of different ways of moving.	1. "Move around the gym in any direction you like."	1. Pupils showed an increasing awareness of space, ways of moving, directions, levels etc.
Questions and answers Problem-solving Guided discovery Teacher-directed	How to create a sequence	2. How to create a sequence: how to start; how to finish; what to put in between.	2. This joint team effort involved the use of the blackboard to examine and analyse the meaning of the term *sequence*, its component parts, linking movements and flow — and what to look for in a good sequence.
Reciprocal Teacher-directed	Performance of a joint sequence	3. "Help your partner to perform the following sequence: start position — travel — jump — roll — balance (three points; symmetrical) — mystery move (your own choice) — finish position." (Assistance provided in *helpful hints* — ie what to look for in a good sequence.)	3. Pupils generally worked enthusiastically and with a little more confidence than in previous sequence work. They had possibly benefited from a return to basics in the previous item (see point 2 above), and had also built up a whole vocabulary of movements. Most "teachers" had difficulty in refining the mystery move (an unknown quantity in the sequence), maybe because they were lacking in movement vocabulary and their eyes were not yet sufficiently trained. Pupils with reading problems continued to find the language too difficult. More careful thought was needed in the preparation of worksheets, in consultation with our remedial department.
Reciprocal teaching	Forward roll	4. "Using your worksheet, help your partner to perform a forward roll."	4. The pupils were much happier and more confident when using a specific worksheet relating to a specific movement. (The forward roll was of course a revision of previous work.)
Reciprocal teaching	Shoulder roll	5. "Using your worksheet, help your partner to perform a shoulder roll."	5. The shoulder roll was a new movement. But the specific nature of the technique, along with the exploded illustrations in the worksheets, helped the pupils to succeed more readily than with a sequence of movements, both as teachers and as performers. It was, however, noted that the quality of the worksheets was fundamental to the success of the strategy.

4.2 Case Study 2

High Park & Coseley Schools, Dudley
Teachers: Roy Anderson, Julie Dignon, Ian Spode

General Aims

The main general objective was to develop personal responsibility and communication skills by means of reciprocal teaching. This was to be achieved by highlighting the pupils' responsibility for themselves, their environment, the equipment and for learning and teaching, and by developing their ability to communicate with staff and peers, both verbally and non-verbally, in relation to specific criteria.

Reconnaissance

The project arose from a specific need for better understanding and methodology in PE teaching, and for the improvement and assessment of personal and social development.

For a number of years we had been interested in producing meaningful and accurate profiles, based not only on physical abilities but also on the child's ability to relate to others in ever-changing circumstances.

We had tried many ways to achieve this, but had always felt that we were failing. Either the result was not accurate enough or it was far too time-consuming for regular use. The teaching styles selected often did not relate to the social aims of our department.

However, after much thought and searching, we realised that the reciprocal style of teaching might go some way towards solving our problem. Reciprocal teaching claimed to highlight the so-called hidden curriculum while giving children the chance to experience an alternative role — that of being an effective facilitator in the learning process.

We had intended to run the project side by side at the same school with similar groups of children. Unfortunately this was not to be, as all the staff involved were promoted — two of them to different schools. It was decided to continue the project but at our new schools. Mrs Dignon would work with a second-year girls' group, while Mr Anderson and Mr Spode would work with a second-year mixed group.

All the participating staff had experienced very traditional training, and had worked for years within formal departments. Mr Anderson, a mature entrant into the profession, had experience of teaching as a member of one department, whilst Mrs Dignon and Mr Spode had both worked in three schools. Our interest in personal development had been fuelled by TVEI-related residential courses, and we appreciated how we could foster these aims through adventure activities and reviewing skills. We felt we could provide similar experience for children within our basic curricular teaching.

We decided to work with first-year groups, anticipating that children with little previous experience would be more willing to adapt to new ideas and teaching methods. However, this decision was somewhat complicated by the age discrepancy between entrants to High Park School, who transferred at eleven, and those to Coseley School, who began at twelve.

Realising that it would be in our own interest to work with children of a similar age (twelve), we decided to work with second-years at High Park and the incoming year at Coseley. The children from High Park had been together as a class, and during that time had experienced active tutorial work, while the children from Coseley only came together for PE and some other practical sessions.

It was vital for us to complete the project by Easter 1987. We were all in new situations, either running departments or on secondment for the autumn term, so we were under pressure to plan, run and evaluate the project within a ten-week period.

Rationale

If one accepts that education should be concerned with a child's personal, social and cognitive development, then subject teachers must by definition recognise the responsibility they have towards the child's whole development. Education should have a cumulatively positive influence on every pupil, and it is the teacher's task to ensure that this happens.

Aims

The aims of the project were to develop the children's competence, both in basketball and in physical education generally, and to develop certain specific motor skills. The aims can be summarised as follows:

- teaching the skills of the set shot, the jump-shot and the one-step lay-up;

- increasing each child's understanding and acceptance of individual differences;

- increasing the children's respect for one another;

- improving the children's self-image — ie raising their expectations and feelings about themselves in relation to PE and basketball specifically.

Objectives

We were specifically interested in the development of:

- communication skills

- a personal sense of responsibility.

We aimed to achieve this by effecting a positive influence on pupils' social awareness by means of activities that would involve:

- sharing

- cooperation

- care of people and equipment

- awareness of individual differences.

How these experiences were presented had to reflect our aims and objectives. We therefore had to teach in a way which would ensure that:

- good relationships were formed, both between the teacher and the pupils and between the pupils themselves;

- pupils learned to understand and cope with certain feelings they experienced, through shared discussion;

- pupils became aware of the changing and contrasting roles they would have to play;

- emphasis was always placed on each individual's worth.

Project Details

The groups

These included one group of 16 girls from High Park School, and two mixed-sex groups of 20 pupils from Coseley School. All were of mixed physical ability and between 12 and 13 years of age.

Period of study

Each group was given five 40-minute lessons over the period from 14 January to 10 April 1987.

Lesson structure

All three teachers worked to a similar lesson format, but each chose his or her own method of achieving the agreed objectives after discussions at weekly meetings (see diary).

Each lesson began with a period of free practice, in which the children could make use of the equipment provided without specific teacher intervention.

This was followed by a period during which the teacher organised a communication game, a sharing exercise

an easy transition into the reciprocal style of teaching.

Each teacher introduced reciprocal teaching in a different way. Mrs Dignon asked the children to identify the social behaviour that was needed when working with a partner as a group exercise. Mr Anderson used a question-and-answer technique to introduce the roles. Mr Spode used wall-charts to emphasise the main points (examples of these can be seen on video recordings).

The final part of the lesson was either an extension of the reciprocal work or a game designed to enhance work already covered.

Reciprocal Teaching

It was an important part of the project to define what we understood about reciprocal teaching. In the reciprocal mode the teacher only communicates directly with the pupil-teacher on the way he/she is giving feedback on the skill to the performer. All information relating to the skill is given to the performer by the pupil-teacher.

This information can be given in many ways. We chose to use task-cards to help the pupil-teacher, but we could have used a demonstration, the blackboard, a video recording or a verbal description.

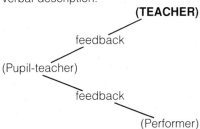

(TEACHER)

feedback

(Pupil-teacher)

feedback

(Performer)

This style of teaching by its very nature fulfils a socialising role. It promotes a new kind of relationship among learners. It encourages patience and tolerance, provides practice in feedback techniques (both giving and receiving), and most importantly helps in the development of respect for the observer's honesty. Immediate feedback from the observer greatly facilitates the traditional learning process in relation to the task itself — though the extent to which this is true depends very much on the accuracy of the feedback.

Monitoring the Project

It was decided to use a variety of techniques in order to analyse the project. These would enable us to monitor how well the programme had been implemented, and produce evidence of its effects from a variety of alternative viewpoints.

Diaries

These were to be kept on a weekly basis to record our feelings, personal observations and reactions. They were to be used during our weekly meetings when reporting to the other members of the group. This report was to be given before we had analysed the video recordings of the sessions. They were to be regarded as a very personal record of our reflections, and so we decided not to present them in the final package except in a very general way. Their value lay in the way that they focused our thoughts and helped with discussions during the planning and performance stage of the project.

Video recordings

These were to provide a visual record of every session, for use in analysing the teaching style and the children's performances and behaviour. It was hoped that they would give precise feedback on how the facilities and equipment were being used, and how the children worked together, observing and communicating clearly. They might also provide examples of children taking responsibility for themselves and others.

Observations

These were to be made by the person operating the video camera. They could take the form of immediate feedback on a specific situation that might have arisen during the lesson, or they might be in the form of a verbal report on the overall feeling the teacher had on the way the lesson had developed. Although we were concerned with the development of the affective domain, we never lost sight of the fact that every lesson must be balanced and must also be effective in the development of the skill. The observations were primarily concerned with whether we were achieving what we had set out to do.

Running commentaries

These were to be of two kinds:

1. During the period of free practice at the start of every lesson, a verbal record was made on the video sound-track in order to help us focus on what the group was doing.

2. While the lesson was in progress, both the teacher and the camera operator were to look for good examples of practice, use of resources, helping others, responsible behaviour, use of equipment and facilities. This was in order to follow up examples of behaviour which would be of use when writing up the report on the project.

Pupil questionnaires

We decided to ask the pupils to complete a questionnaire at the end of the five sessions. We would use this to get feedback on the way the children had felt during the programme. (Examples of questionnaires used can be found in Chapter 9.)

Figure 4.7 Lesson 1   14 January 1987

Lesson objectives   ● to introduce reciprocal teaching;
● to promote communication and responsibility;
● to introduce the set shot.

Activities	Purpose	Evaluation
Julie Dignon		
1. Five minutes' free practice/discovery.	1. To observe pupils taking responsibility for their own learning and practice.	1. Little skill was shown, but pupils reacted by working in pairs or small groups, not as individuals.
2. Passing: technique, receiving, eye contact.	2. To develop pupils' awareness and passing skills.	2. There was a good response to questions, but pupils lacked an awareness of skill.
3. Pupils used the brainstorm method in groups to bring out important areas of reciprocal teaching, such as teacher and learner roles, observation and responsibility.	3. To observe individual and group communication and give pupils a chance to enhance their own understanding of reciprocal teaching.	3. There was very good group communication and good awareness of reciprocal needs. But pupils did not observe very well, and were poor at praising and encouraging. They felt strange in the role of teacher.
4. Pupils worked on the set shot using task-cards.	4. To observe teacher and learner roles and get an overall impression of how much responsibility has been accepted.	4. Pupils found this difficult to grasp.
5. Competition: how many out of five; one-to-one; pupils' own rules.	5. To develop the pupils' skills in the set shot.	
Roy Anderson		
1. Five minutes' free practice/discovery.	1. To observe pupils taking responsibility for their own learning and practice.	1. It took the form of discovery rather than practice. Pupils clearly lacked any sort of shooting technique.
2. Passing: technique, movement, signal awareness.	2. To develop the chest pass and apply it to game situations.	2. Pupil skills developed well and achieved sound awareness. Little communication or social interaction occurred.
3. Introduction to reciprocal teaching: roles; areas of concern; practice in the set shot.	3. To show the need for honesty, communication etc and to observe the teacher and learner roles.	3. The method was introduced in a confused way. Pupils were unsure of their roles and of the purpose of the activity. Skill development was limited.
4. Game: cross-court; free set shot on mat.	4. To place the set shot within the context of the game.	4. Pupils responded well and became highly involved. Controlled use of skills led to some success.

Figure 4.7 (continued)

Activities	Purpose	Evaluation
Ian Spode		
1. Five minutes' free practice/discovery.	1. To observe pupils taking responsibility for their own learning and practice; to assess their awareness of the game and see how they communicated.	1. Very little concentrated skill practice took place. Discovery was of a very haphazard kind.
2. Verbal identification of skill areas used in basketball.	2. To find out the pupils' awareness of the game and see how they communicated.	2. Pupils had to be drawn out to communicate knowledge.
3. Warm-up: running/dribbling game.	3. To set the tone of the lesson and overcome their fears of a new teacher.	3. Pupils reacted well to a traditional teaching style, but were slow to react to specific questions.
4. Introduction to reciprocal teaching: roles; responsibility, observation, communication; practice in the set shot.	4. To observe pupils in teacher and learner roles, and assess their observational powers and acceptance of responsibility.	4. Pupils were generally unable to communicate about skill. Their comments were irrelevant, and they showed poor observation of their partners.
5. Shooting game in pairs.	5. To enhance pupils' awareness of their skills of observation and judgement, highlighting trust and honesty.	5. Pupils lacked these skills, though their activity and the summing-up made them aware of this.
6. Summming up the lesson with the pupils.		

Figure 4.8   Basketball: The Set Shot

This shot is performed one-handed, standing still.

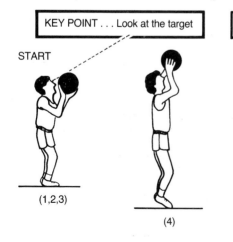

KEY POINT . . . Look at the target

START

(1,2,3)

(4)

Keep the ball high.

FINISH

(5)

IMPORTANT
The helper must check the following points each time a shot is practised:

1. Hold the ball in your best hand
   (fingers pointing towards your forehead).

2. Place the other hand at the side of the ball
   (for support).

3. Stand with your feet a shoulder-width apart and
   your knees bent.

4. Push the ball upwards and forwards at the
   target (release with a flick of the wrist).

5. Straighten the legs
   (to give power to the shot).

Figure 4.9 Lesson 2   4 February 1987

Lesson objectives
- to highlight the need to take personal responsibility;
- to enhance communication skills;
- to develop skill in the jump shot.

Activities	Purpose	Evaluation
Julie Dignon		
1. Five minutes' free practice.	1. As in Lesson 1.	1. Little actual learning took place.
2. Communication game: passing the ball in a circle.	2. To encourage pupils to say positive things about each other.	2. Shouting of words took away inhibitions.
3. Recap and improvement on previous work.	3. To get pupils to suggest more ideas to increase understanding.	3. Pupils were not so forthcoming to add words to the chart.
4. The jump shot, using a task-card.	4. To continue the teacher and learner roles.	4. Skill levels improved, but the task-card proved difficult to understand.
5. Verbal re-emphasis of teacher and learner roles: observation, praise etc	5. To bring these aspects into teacher and learner roles.	5. Observation was poor.
6. Dribble and shoot exercise.	6. To encourage pupil observation.	
7. Two-against-one game	7. To increase the awareness of skill.	7. Pupils found the game hard to understand.
Roy Anderson		
1. Five minutes' free practice.	1. The same as before.	1. A great deal of individual work of a haphazard nature.
2. Communication exercise: name-calling.	2. To increase communication between pupils.	2. Very good responses and good communication.
3. The group was questioned on the reciprocal work of the previous week.	3. To clarify the previous week's work, discuss problems and enhance pupils' awareness of their roles.	3. Pupils were now more aware of what was expected.
4. The jump shot using a task-sheet.	4. To observe pupils in teacher and learner roles.	4. Performance was generally good, though observation could have been better.
5. Pairs game: five shots outscore partner; either set or jump shot.	5. For pupils to discover their success level with each shot.	5. Pupils were able to distinguish between both shots.
6. Games: two across court; encourage getting into shooting position.	6. For pupils to recognise when and when not to shoot.	6. There was a mixed reaction but some skill in shooting.

Figure 4.9 (continued)

Activities	Purpose	Evaluation
Ian Spode		
1. Five minutes' free practice.	1. The same as before.	1. Technique was poor, and little learning or practice took place.
2. Three-against-one game: passing/shooting.	2. To recognise how and where to pass, when and where to shoot, and to develop team cooperation.	2. There was little success with team help and cooperation.
3. Defence positions.	3. For pupils to understand where they should stand.	3. Pupils responded as individuals rather than as a team.
4. Jump shot, using a task-sheet.	4. To observe pupils and encourage praise and attention to detail.	4. Pupils took responsibility for their own defence.
5. Three-against-one game.	5. For players to know when to shoot, and for the defender to prevent the shot.	5. Pupils lacked observation and were unable to take the teaching role seriously.
6. Summing-up.	6. Mainly for pupils to take responsibility for the equipment and for themselves.	6. Pupils were encouraged to accept their own responsibility for learning, but continued to show a poor attitude.

Figure 4.10   Basketball: The Jump Shot

This shot is performed in the air, shooting in a similar manner to the set shot.

KEY POINT . . . shoot at the top of the jump.

Hold the ball in a similar way
to the set shot.
Shoot at the top of the jump.

Two bounces into
the shooting area;
bend the knees to
control the stop.

Keep the ball high.

Jump straight up,
and extend the arm and
elbow towards the
basket.

WATCH THE TARGET

FINISH

Extend the arm and
hand towards the target,
and follow through with a
limp wrist.

Figure 4.11 Lesson 3 11 February 1987

| Lesson objectives | ● to increase pupils' awareness of responsibility; |
| | ● to introduce the one-step lay-up. |

Activities	Purpose	Evaluation
Julie Dignon		
1. Free practice.	1. As in Lesson 1.	1. Spasmodic practice of previous shots.
2. Passing game in fours: pass and follow.	2. A challenge situation to encourage passing skills.	2– The work was too complex, so there was 4. little success. The pupils were very negative about all three games.
3. Three against one, passing only.	3. To encourage efficiency and quick passing.	
4. Three against one, with shooting.	4. Only using the jump shot — pupils to manoeuvre into position for shot.	
5. One-step lay-up, using task-card.	5. To encourage detailed observation of shots.	5. The task-card confused the pupils, as it could be interpreted in many different ways.
6. Three-against-one game, using only the lay-up.	6. To place the lay-up into the context of a game.	6. There was no time for a game at the end.
Roy Anderson		
1. Free practice.	1. As in Lesson 1.	1. Pupils showed responsibility for their own learning.
2. Communication exercise.	2. Changing groups to encourage rapid communication.	2. Pupils were all successful at communicating with each other.
3. Three against one: ten passes, then a shot.	3. Efficient passing to release the shot.	3. The group cooperated well, taking responsibility for counting.
4. Key points covered from the lay-up sheet.	4. For pupils to communicate key points.	4. Recognition of key points avoided confusion in this technique.
5. Pupils followed a leader in a pairs competition, with the choice of shot up to the leader.	5. To encourage the following pupil to be honest in recognising shots.	5. Some pupils were not completely honest, but owned up on questioning.
6. Cross-court game.	6. Winners to play each other to encourage team cooperation.	6. The game showed a good skill level and good team cooperation.

Figure 4.11 (continued)

Activities	Purpose	Evaluation
Ian Spode		
1. Free practice.	1. As in Lesson 1.	1. Some methodical practice was now being seen.
2. Questioning to identify foot patterns for effective jumping.	2. For pupils to recognise the most efficient methods in relation to individual shots.	2. The group was slow to come up with answers.
3. Lifting skills in threes.	3. Fun activity to encourage observation and communication.	3. There was plenty of involvement and good communication.
4. Three-against-one game.		
5. The lay-up, using the task-card.	5. To encourage pupils to make very detailed observations.	5. Lack of observation meant reduced skill development.
6. Three-against-one game.	6. For pupils to practise the shots they were most happy with.	6. There was more cooperation towards the end, as they began to accept group responsibility.

Figure 4.12   Basketball: The One-step Lay-up Shot

This shot is performed on the move. It can be made either from a pass or a dribble

TARGET AREA
Try to push the ball into the corner of the small square marked on the backboard.

KEY POINT . . . POSITION
Approach the basket at 45 degrees.

45°   45°

4. Jump high and reach for the target pushing the ball onto the backboard with your right hand.

3. Step forward onto your left foot.

2. Look at the target.

1. Hold the ball in both hands with your feet a shoulder-width apart.

START

Figure 4.13 Lesson 4 18 February 1987

Lesson objectives	● to bring together the shots that had been learned;
	● to develop the skills into a game;
	● to increase communication.

Activities	Purpose	Evaluation
Julie Dignon		
1. Five minutes' free practice/ discovery.	1. To observe pupils taking responsibility for their own learning and practice.	1. Pupils took greater responsibility for all learning and practised shooting.
2. Dribbling: low and high; right-hand and left-hand.	2. To develop pupils' ability to handle the ball and awareness of space.	2. Skills were more thorough than before. Pupils responded well to dribbling.
3. The same again, keeping contact with ball and trying to break other people's contact.		3. Pupils were lively, developing good skills.
4. Pairs discover their respective personal best shot, scoring 2 for a basket and 1 for good technique.	4. To improve the pupil-teacher's observation so that he could identify his own ability and that of his partner — and to encourage honesty.	4. Pupils took responsibility well, choosing task-cards, looking at wall charts, and being helpful to each other.
5. Three against one: passing, dribbling and choosing when to shoot.	5. To identify when to use which shot, and develop a cooperative game.	5. Awareness of the game was improving.
Roy Anderson		
1. Five minutes' free practice/discovery.	1. To observe pupils taking responsibility for their own learning and practice.	1. There was much more activity, with pupils working together to improve skill.
2. Teacher demonstration of ball-handling skills, copied by pupils.	2. To introduce different practices for hand/ eye coordination.	2. There was a good response, with useful observation and copying.
3. Pupils to make up their own practices and matches.	3. Pupils had to take responsibility for their own learning and to communicate with each other.	3. Good skill development and cooperation.
4. Three cones at different distances from basket — which shot to use?	4. To introduce discovery learning, in which pupils must think and relate knowledge to each other.	4. Good problem-solving on the part of pupils.
5. Two cross-court games; three circles drawn around target. Free shot, using the correct shot.	5. To bring problem-solving into the game situation and encourage the use of the correct technique.	5. Pupils were a little uncontrolled in skills, as they were under pressure to be correct.

Figure 4.13 Lesson 4 (continued)

Activities	Purpose	Evaluation
Ian Spode		
1. Five minutes' free practice/discovery.	1. To observe pupils taking responsibility for their own learning and practice.	1. There was good overall pupil interaction; skills were practised well and a small game was played.
2. Dribbling: small game in restricted area. Dribbling into shooting: what is the best place to shoot from?	2. To improve ball-handling skills and introduce a problem-solving situation.	2. There was a good lively beginning, but pupils found difficulty in identifying the angle of approach.
3. Reciprocal teaching: identifying the best shot and practising with a partner.	3. To improve pupil-teacher observation and to identify personal achievement.	3. Pupils showed good responsibility and perseverance.
4. Two against one: the best place to shoot from; the best place to defend.	4. For pupils to relate shots to the game in a questioning session.	4. Pupils still needed prompting from the teacher in order to observe the correct places.
5. Tournament using teams of three.	5. To use learned skills in the game.	5. Pupils cooperated well, displaying a good attitude.

Figure 4.14 Lesson 5 4 March 1987

Lesson objectives
- to incorporate the shots which had been learned into the game technique;
- to continue to develop communication skills.

Activities	Purpose	Evaluation
Ian Spode		
1. Five minutes' free practice/discovery.	1. To observe pupils taking responsibility for their own learning and practice.	1. There was no excitement, but crowding at baskets. A two-against-one game developed.
2. Identifying the weakest shot.	2. To allow individual pupils to recognise their own ability.	2/3. Pupils had difficulty identifying their weak shot. This created tension and was not successful.
3. Reciprocal teaching of the weakest shot.	3. To help partners improve their ability.	
4. Games in teams of three, with emphasis on travelling and double-dribble violations.	4. To introduce the rules of basketball.	4. The class attitude deteriorated. The teacher needed to lay emphasis on acceptable behaviour, responsibility and self-control.
5. Games for understanding, including possession and shooting where possible.	5. To compel pupils to think about their actions.	
Roy Anderson		
1. Five minutes' free practice/discovery.	1. To observe pupils taking responsibility for their own learning and practice.	1. Pupils worked well in pairs. One pair of pupils worked on a new ball-handling sequence.
2. Passing in pairs, emphasising the pivot, turning away from partner.	2. To introduce a new skill related to movement with the ball.	2. Work was too complicated and too incoherent.
3. In pairs: score as many baskets as possible in three minutes.	3. To encourage competition for action and use of shots.	3. Pupils did not work as expected, as they had difficulty grasping the practice.
4. Drill: how to make up a shooting drill.	4. To develop problem-solving, cooperation and discussion.	4. The pupils worked together well, taking an interest in the task and providing some good ideas.
5. Two cross-court games.	5. The development of pivot and shooting.	5. The pupils cooperated and performed well.

Julie Dignon   No lesson — school late opening.

Benefits of Reciprocal Teaching

There are many advantages and some disadvantages for both teacher and pupil when using this teaching method. These are listed below, based on our own experiences during the project and on video analysis made after the event.

Positive enhancement of skill

This was the most striking feature of reciprocal teaching. Pupils gained a great deal from being constantly involved at all times, both cognitively and actively. A particularly large improvement was observed in the specific technique of closed shooting, although this did not stand up in the context of open situations. Many examples can be seen on the video to support this point.

Better pupil–pupil communication

The very nature of reciprocal teaching means that pupils must communicate with each other, and should improve their communication skills through practice and guidance from the teacher. However, it was very difficult to come to any firm conclusions in this area. Pupils communicated about specific matters, gave feedback and helped each other, but it was impossible to tell what level of improvement had been achieved. But we all thought we had made progress in this area by demonstrating ways of initiating and forming working relationships.

Better pupil–teacher communication

This area showed a marked improvement. Children initiated communication, not only about the psychomotor aspects of the lesson, but also about their feelings. We have not experienced this to such a great extent in any of our earlier teaching, and we felt that this must be directly attributable to the style selected.

Improved self-esteem

We thought this should have improved thanks to the constant positive feedback being given to the children by both the teacher and the other pupils. Unfortunately, without a self-concept test we have no way of assessing if any improvement was made. We all feel that reciprocal teaching must have a positive influence in this area, and would continue to use it as we believe it to be of benefit to the children.

Longer periods of active learning

This was one of the major benefits we found from reciprocal teaching. Children spent more time on each task with constant feedback, although this was at times of a dubious nature. For the teaching of closed skills we all felt that this method did produce excellent results, and would be of use whether or not the social domain was being highlighted.

Problems Associated with Reciprocal Teaching

1. Both children and teachers found the transition from formal traditional teaching difficult. The reciprocal method required far more from the pupils, and many found this threatening. They found problems with the lack of teacher feedback. The teachers found it very difficult to move from giving feedback on the activity to giving feedback on the observational and teaching skills. This required quite a shift in our teaching behaviour, as we tended to focus in on the activity.

2. We found it difficult to communicate with the observers only. Often we were drawn towards helping with the skill, which would be our normal role.

3. We felt that reciprocal teaching should be limited to carefully selected situations, and should only be used for short periods during any lesson. Pupils soon lost interest in the skill, especially when they were having difficulties.

4. We felt that reciprocal teaching should be limited to the development of closed skills, because it was very difficult to use for the acquisition of open skills.

5. The feedback that was given was often not accurate enough, so that pupils found it difficult to progress beyond a very basic stage. This compounded the problems caused by difficulties in reading and in remembering specific points from the task-cards, so that teacher intervention was often the only solution.

6. Development of the task-cards must be an ongoing process related to individual pupils' needs and abilities. We experienced many difficulties with the cards, and in future we would try to simplify them as much as possible.

Conclusions

The project obviously highlighted areas of social development through the very nature of the reciprocal role. Pupils communicated better, both with the teachers and with their peers, and took greater responsibility for their own progress and that of their peers. We cannot predict what further developments will occur in this area, but it is likely that relationships and social behaviour will continue to improve.

However, it is very important to remember that there are many influences on children's social behaviour. These include home background, family relationships, environment, experiences at school and the influence of peers and of the media. The teacher cannot change these factors, but can only influence them by suggesting or introducing certain types of acceptable behaviour. In our project we have seen a small part of this influencing process through the use of reciprocal teaching. We feel that, with carefully selected use over a long period, it could become a useful tool in the social development of the child.

It could also be used in many other subject areas, enabling children to take responsibility for their own learning and that of their peers under the guidance of their teacher.

It is interesting to note after the completion of the project that this style of teaching has had a positive influence on all the teachers. It has made us more aware of the personal and social needs of the pupils, and we are all consciously adjusting our styles of teaching to accommodate to these needs. As for the children who took part in the project, we can refer them back to the reciprocal style and instruct them to help their partners in many diverse teaching situations.

With selective use, reciprocal teaching can provide a beneficial means for teacher and pupil to develop communication skills and social awareness. It is an ongoing process which, once initiated, can be slowly built upon, encouraging more trust between teacher and pupils and between the pupils themselves.

5. CASE STUDY 3: INCLUSION STYLE

5.1 Case Study 3

Kimberworth Comprehensive School, Rotherham
Class: 1st-year Swimming
Teacher: John Gray

General Introduction

Taking part in the National Study Group proved to be successful in our department for many reasons:

1. We decided to work together as a department in order to examine different aspects of our teaching style.

2. This promoted more discussion and meetings within the department than had been the case in the past.

3. We were all able to observe at least one member of the department while being involved in the project.

4. Two members of the department had the opportunity of teaching a group as a team.

5. It meant that more planning and preparation were needed for each lesson.

The styles that we decided to try out were the reciprocal approach for cricket and gymnastics and the inclusion style for swimming. The third of these projects is dealt with in more detail below.

General Conclusions

As a department we felt that we were very didactic in our approach. We did use other styles of teaching, such as inclusion and guided discovery, but were not totally aware of this at the time.

The project has made us all more aware of our teaching styles, and has also enabled pupils to participate in the execution of their lesson. They were totally involved in the lessons, and were able to give their partners sufficient teaching points in order to perform basic balancing skills. Both pupil and staff observation were much greater during the course of the project. The pupils observed each other, and this enabled the teacher to observe more pupils than is normally possible in a lesson.

It is difficult to evaluate how successful the various teaching styles were, because we have nothing to compare them with. However, if the main aim is to improve the children's participation along with all the other objectives listed earlier in this project, then it has undoubtedly been successful.

If we are to carry on looking more closely at our teaching styles, then

"One hundred pupils filled in questionnaires. Eighty-one pupils enjoyed the freedom of choice of entry into a skill, therefore determining their own level and success."

"There is a difficulty relating to some pupils' inability to perceive their actual level of attainment and to set realistic goals."

we need to be even more specific about our overall aims and objectives; a lot more preparation will be involved, and the work should not just be confined to one specific group.

Using the Inclusion Style in the Front Crawl

Aim

To examine the merits of an inclusion style of teaching in swimming.

Objectives

● to develop good technique in front crawl;

● to involve pupils more in their own learning;

● to give pupils an opportunity to assess their own learning and ability;

● to teach all pupils as individuals, so that each is given choices within the overall framework.

Procedures

The work of eight groups of first-year swimmers was developed in the following way:

● four groups were taught according to the inclusion style;

● the other four groups were taught as normal to provide a control.

There were approximately twenty pupils in each group. John Gray and the swimming classes were observed by K. Swift and by as many of the PE department as could be released for the purpose (some were needed to observe other classes).

Evaluation involved the subjective analysis of groups:

● How the control and inclusion groups developed.

● How the children worked using different styles.

● How the control groups were being taught.

● Observation over a period of four weeks.

● Discussions on work evaluation.

The approach to be used

The slanting-rope principle of the inclusion style.

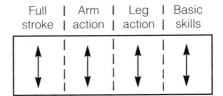

| Full stroke | Arm action | Leg action | Basic skills |

1. The pool was divided into four areas, each for working on the aspect indicated.

2. Entry into area was the decision of each pupil.

3. The breakdown of work into skills practices was based on each pupil's assessment of himself.

4. Each pupil was able to assess his own progress and move on to the next part of the task.

5. Pupils needed to be given points to concentrate on in their work, such as knee and ankle movement in the kick. This meant that the self-check style had also to be included.

Evaluation

1. The project proved to be a successful method of teaching over the four-week period:

● Pupils commented on how they enjoyed the work.

● There was a relaxed atmosphere.

● The pupils worked well.

● There were many instances of pupils asking for help rather than being spoon-fed.

2. There appeared to be no significant differences in technical development between the inclusion groups and the control groups.

3. The inclusion groups became more involved in decision-making and were more aware of their strengths and weaknesses.

4. Some of the better pupils found the style easy to adapt to.

However...

5. Many of the poorer swimmers had no concept of how to make decisions about their own styles. For example, one awful swimmer tried to join the top group, and thought he was right to do so.

6. Some of the better pupils needed more specific coaching than the project could afford.

Questions raised

1. Is it beneficial for children to be more aware of their standard and progress in learning?

2. If so, can a system such as this operate in isolation, or should it be part of an overall school teaching method?

3. How long does it take for the slow learner to develop the skills that this teaching style requires?

4. Is there any benefit for the child who has already developed a good standard of work?

6. CASE STUDY 4: GUIDED DISCOVERY STYLE

6.1 Case Study 4

Alumwell Community School, Walsall
Class: 1st-year dancing
Teacher: Jackie Callicott

Project Details

Time available

Six weeks with one 45-minute lesson per week.

Facilities

Gym/dance studio

Class profile

The class was a first-year mixed-ability group of 16 pupils aged between 11 and 12. Their actual ability was not known at first, but after the first lesson it became apparent that the range was mixed low to average.

Experience

This was mostly very little. By show of hands we discovered that the pupils come from a variety of junior schools, and many had no experience of creative work at all. Two pupils did not speak English.

The pupils were typical of the school as a whole in that they came from a variety of cultural and racial backgrounds. Muslim girls were taking part for the first time.

Teaching theme

Introduction to body awareness and action vocabulary for travelling.

Aims

1. To look at the teaching strategies that make up the guided discovery style:

   ● to see if it can be clearly distinguished as a style;

   ● to see if it can be used to achieve a particular objective, with the pupils directing the pace of work and the direction for each week's progression.

2. To investigate any factors that guided discovery may influence:

   ● group or pair work and social development;

   ● developing the quality of work (fine motor skills);

   ● enabling pupils to retain information from one week to the next.

Figure 6.1 Dance Notes Diary: Lesson 1

Theme: Body awareness
Objectives: Introduction to dance; pupil response

Strategy used	Work covered	Outcome
Guided Discovery	1. Movement around the floor; use of space; feet travelling.	1. Pupils had no idea what was going on, and needed more explanation.
	2. Concentrating on the space covered when moving: floor, walls etc.	
Didactic Interference	3. Choosing the body part to move.	3. Space was discussed; pupils reacted well but chose hands only.
	4. The teacher showed how part of the body leads in space and naturally involves the whole body.	4. The lesson became more creative.
	5. Pupils used hands, knees and back to lead the movement, and started to use space and different levels, although this was not discussed at this point.	5. The pupils started to travel using the whole body.
	6. A short phrase was built up.	
Comments	This was a difficult group and needed a lot of teacher guidance. They were not used to creative work. There was also some language difficulty: a word like "fine" meant nothing to many of them.	

Figure 6.2 Dance Notes Diary: Lesson 2

Theme: Action vocabulary
Objectives: Body awareness, concentrating on travelling (how and where)

Strategy used	Work covered	Outcome
Guided discovery	1. Warm-up: moving all parts of the body to a fast beat.	1. Pupils made a good start and responded well to music; little intervention was needed when they were challenged with music.
	2. Different speed and direction of movement; different gestures; firm, strong, fast, slow; making an imprint use of percussion.	2. Pupils responded well to a different stimulus, and found it easier to move.
	3. Short sequence: travel, shape; starting and stopping a turn etc; thinking about floor pattern.	3. The sequences worked out well compared with the first week.
Comments	It was difficult to assess whether guided discovery was having an effect, or whether the pupils were simply more relaxed with having music to work from.	

Figure 6.3 Dance Notes Diary: Lesson 3

Theme: Action vocabulary
Objective: To build up a movement phrase using pathways

Strategy used	Work covered	Outcome
Teacher-directed	1. Fast warm-up with music; repeat of exeercise in use of floor space.	1. There was a good start again.
Guided discovery	2. Floor pattern using letters: each pupil to think about the shape of a letter.	
	3. Words used to move to, such as "long", "point" and "sharp"; everyone tried these movements.	3. Pupils responded well to words used such as "sharp", "round" and "angle". There was better social interaction, and pupils realised they could talk.
	4. A short movement phrase was built up using floor pattern and words, and a guessing game was played.	4. This worked well.
Comments	Once pupils were given the chance to discuss, they were much happier to show their work, and now appeared to have settled. However, they still responded very differently to the teacher-directed warm-up.	

Figure 6.4 Dance Notes Diary: Lesson 4

Theme: Travelling
Objective: Action vocabulary (continuation)

Strategy used	Work covered	Outcome
Didactic	1. Warm-up: travelling directions and use of floor space.	1. The start was very quiet, and a great deal of recap was needed.
Brain-storming	2. Use of the words "skip", "hop", "jump", and ways to travel.	2. Pupils came up with their own words, and showed greater understanding.
Guided discovery	3. Which direction? — how?	3. Pupils started to use their whole bodies. They used touch, became more imaginative and started to enjoy themselves more.
Guided discovery	4. Pupils worked in pairs on three words to move to, using their own initiative and developing the word sequence.	4. Pupils moved according to their own words, including turning, moving along diagonals, size of movement was related to the words selected.
Comments	Pupils got much more from this session, picking out relevant work and developing their own ideas. One pupil took the word "role" and used it to travel.	

Figure 6.5 Dance Notes Diary: Lesson 5

Theme: Travelling
Objective: To put together methods of travelling and to introduce pair work

Strategy used	Work covered	Outcome
Didactic	1. Recap of words and ways of moving such as glide, roll, pattern, stamp etc.	1. Pupils starting to pick up ideas much more quickly, and were remembering things.
Guided discovery	2. Choice of direction.	2. Pupils experimented well, using walls and different levels (although this had not as yet been covered).
Problem-solving	3. Pupils were put in pairs and given a directive: "Make an interesting pattern with changes of movement."	3. All sorts of things came out of this: mirroring, opposites, use of small and large spaces and touching.
Guided discovery	4. Experimentation on how to "use" a partner when travelling.	4. There were some good sequences, with much discussion going on.
Didactic	5. Discussion on what happened.	
Comments	Work from the last four weeks had been remembered, and the opportunity to "use" a partner for ideas made many of the pupils feel more relaxed about "dancing". As always it was interesting to note who was leading.	

Figure 6.6 Dance Notes Diary: Lesson 6

Theme: Travelling/Body awareness
Objective: To finalise work and go over what makes a good sequence or phrase.

Strategy used	Work covered	Outcome
Guided discovery	1. Free movement to music.	1. Pupils were much better behaved and more relaxed, and one or two were impatient to start the lesson proper. Most were happy and enjoying the prospect.
Discussion/didactic	2. Further work on travel, use of space and shape.	2. Pupils were enthusiastic and remembered more of their work. They used ideas taken from demonstration in previous lessons.
Guided discovery	3. Development of a sequence, adding more ideas and encouraging creativity, eg in the use of the floor and of a partner.	
Comments	The last two weeks had shown pleasing progress, The pupils' enthusiasm had increased, and they were more relaxed and as a result more creative. It had taken a while for information to "stick" from week to week, but the group's creativity level had been raised considerably from virtually nil thanks to this method of teaching.	

Teacher's General Summary

At the beginning I was not sure of how to isolate this strategy. I decided that thorough planning was needed and wrote copious notes. By the end of the first lesson, however, I realised that this was pointless, as the pupils were directing the pace of the lesson. So although I continued to plan, the follow-up became more important.

The members of this particular teaching group were fairly inhibited and shy. The first week it was hard to get them to talk, and they didn't appear to have much background in creative work. So I plodded on!

By week three I had some information to start looking at, and was getting a response from the pupils. I did find, however, that as soon as the pupils looked confused or inhibited I immediately switched to a different strategy. I was still doing a great deal of teacher-directed work and question-and-answer sessions, but I was also becoming more confident with the concept of guided discovery.

In week four I invited some colleagues in to help identify what strategy I was using, and found that by this time I seemed to have got it sorted out. The teaching notes above show that the pupils were guiding me and we got where I wanted them to go.

Lessons five and six were much more lively, and most things had been covered by the end of the block of work.

Conclusions

1. The group started slowly, and normally I would have used a teacher-directed approach with them.

2. The quality of the work improved only slowly, but the creativity level was higher in the end.

3. I did not allow much room for social interaction — only pairs. So the course was very individually based from the point of view of social interaction.

4. Towards the end of the block the pupils' memory was improving.

5. Pupils did become more confident as they realised their own ideas were of value.

The future

I will take another group of children and continue to look at guided discovery as a teaching strategy. This work has made me very aware of my own teaching styles in other lessons. I found this group quite introverted as new first years. The next group, I hope, will have settled in a lot more, and may respond differently.

7. CASE STUDIES 5 & 6: PROBLEM-SOLVING STYLE

7.1 Case Study 5

Leamore JMI School, Walsall
Teaching for understanding
Class: Junior 4 (mixed/mixed ability)
Teacher: Sue Orton

Aim

1. To explore and investigate three named strategies.

2. By detailed planning, implementation and evaluation of each strategy, to be able to identify what contribution each can make to children's development.

3. Following the outcome of this, to examine the possibilities for disseminating the results within the LEA in order to assist teachers in becoming more effective in their role.

Objectives

To explore an understanding approach to teaching games, and attempt to assess its contribution towards cognitive, social, psychomotor and personal development.

My Strategy

My approach was varied, but laid emphasis on the following aspects:

● problem-solving;

● creativity;

● understanding the concept of the game.

I also explored the effects of the strategy on:

● the teacher (ie myself);

● the pupils as perceived by the teacher.

(I also propose to explore the pupils' own perception of their progress, but have not done so as yet.)

Effects on the Teacher

1. Investigation has given me a clearer awareness of my own strategy and those of my colleagues.

2. I have been able to explore the wider implications and potential of the strategy. When previously using this strategy, I may have tended to switch to another strategy, whereas persistence on this occasion produced the desired outcome in that pupils solved their own problems without any premature intervention by the teacher.

3. The understanding approach relies heavily on a sensitive teacher who knows the children well, and who will intervene at the appropriate moment. Guidance to a

"Their responses showed an understanding of the games far beyond that which I thought they were capable of."

"Pupils thought more about what actions were being taken and why, rather than just doing things."

"Some children found it difficult to make a decision. It is important to involve the whole group, and you must be aware of individual strengths and weaknesses."

"Children were better able to function at their own level."

"The understanding approaoch (problem-solving) caters for cognitive, social and personal development. The psychomotor aspects tend to be less well provided for."

solution is better than direction without real understanding. The children must understand why they are doing what they are doing.

4. It prompted me to do a comparison of what an understanding approach had to offer as opposed to a skill-based or traditional approach. Could one approach offer more to a wider audience than the other?

5. The structure of games is important for children to understand, and it is difficult for them to distinguish between the concepts of competition and cooperation.

Effects on the Pupils
(from the teacher's point of view)

1. More children were actively involved, with greater participation.

2. Pupils thought more about what actions were being taken and why, rather than just doing things.

3. During the course pupils became more imaginative in their thinking and ideas.

4. Pupils who had previously been passive were now starting to be more confident in front of their peers — wanting to demonstrate ideas, and wanting to explain, even if they could not perform the selected activity very well. All the children were wanting to build upon each other's ideas. There was a sharing and pooling of ideas.

5. The strategy is child-centred in its approach.

6. Children were better able to function at their own level. Skill development took place when appropriate to the individual group, and rarely was a class skill taught in isolation.

7. Skills could now be seen in context.

On the negative side ...

8. Skill development was much slower and the few more able children were possibly less well catered for.

Benefits of the Project as a Whole

1. I was given the opportunity to work with, discuss and share ideas with teachers in other LEAs.

2. Discussions with colleagues in my own LEA gave me extra motivation and stimulation.

3. The project highlighted the need for more critical observation of pupil performance and response. This encouraged better observation on my part (it is so easy to become too superficial and base your teaching structure on assumed responses).

4. In the light of a more critical observation, planning has been more structured and more relevant to each child; my work has become more child-centred.

5. Better planning has resulted in a more progressive approach.

6. Evaluation of outcomes and approaches has been more realistic.

Summary of Conclusions

No one strategy can be used in isolation. A balanced mixture of several strategies is more likely to cater for all pupils' needs.

The understanding (problem-solving) approach caters for cognitive, social and personal development. The psychomotor aspects tend to be less well provided for.

Without this teaching style we are in danger of becoming too subject-orientated and uniform in our approach, and of making too many assumptions about our pupils' skill level. Children used to the infant-school approach, that allows them to explore and familiarise themselves with various pieces of equipment, are suddenly thrown into full-scale games with teams of six children or more.

Within this project, pupils have shown an understandable lack of awareness about what constitutes a game, and that the two concepts of cooperation and competition can be dealt with together. The very essence of team games is cooperation first and competition second. Yet how often do we pursue competition first and expect cooperation to follow?

My own survey of skill-based traditional versus an understanding approach showed that the latter catered far better for more children in their all-round development.

Diary

Theme

Teaching for understanding, incorporating creativity and problem-solving.

Class

Junior 4: 35 children of mixed sexes and mixed ability.

Time available

One 40-minute lesson per week over a period of ten weeks (with some weeks off).

Lessons 1 & 2

17 & 24 September 1986

These two weeks were of an exploratory nature with regard to relationships. The children were getting used to a more thought-orientated approach.

I pitched the work at far too high a level, and the children found great difficulty with it. They were unable to cope with the large open spaces on the playing fields, and there were a number of reasons for this.

A more basic approach was therefore adopted for week 3 (see below).

	1 Oct 1986	8 Oct 1986	15 Oct 1986	5 Nov 1986	19 Nov 1986	26 Nov 1986	3 Dec 1986	
Direct/Didactic	*	*	*	*	*	*	*	(Warm up only)
Guided discovery	*		*					
Reciprocal learning								
Understanding	*	*	*	*	*	*	*	
Problem-solving	*	*	*	*	*	*	*	
Creative	*	*		*	*	*	**	
Decision making	*	*		*		*	*	
Individual work	*	*	*	*	*	*	*	
Group work			*	*	*	*	*	
Brainstorming				*	*			
Question/Answer	*	*	*					
Pairs	*	*	*	*	*	*	*	

Figure 7.1 Lesson 3

1 October 1986

Strategy	Work covered	Questions and responses	Outcomes
Teacher-directed	Warm-up: varying foot patterns; vigorous; shuttle.		Warm-up was vigorous, and the method used ensured that pupils listened.
Guided discovery Questions and answers	Discussion	"What makes up a game?" Answers included: "using your brain", "fun", "equipment", "rules".	
Creative	We decided to concentrate on ... [see next column] Working individually, making up a game without equipment.	... rules, brainwork and fun.	Children found this difficult, and missed having equipment or a partner. They decided this was too restricting, but agreed that they had used their brain. They had made up a rule, but it was not really fun.
	Working with a partner, making up a game without equipment, while considering the following points: [see next column]	"Does this make any difference?" "Can you make rules, use your brain — and is it fun?" "Can you make your game into more fun?" "Try it out."	Children made up a variety of games which fulfilled all their requirements. They agreed that adding scoring would make it more fun. This added a new dimension; the pupils became very involved and thoroughly enjoyed their game. Equipment was not essential.

Figure 7.2 Lesson 4

8 October 1986

Strategy	Work covered	Questions and responses	Outcomes
Teacher-directed	Foot patterns: "Simon says".		Warming-up activity.
Creative	Dictate a pattern: 4 x 2 — the rest of the group copy it.		Pupils found difficulty with this type of freedom.
Questions and answers	Revising previous week's thoughts on: [see next column]	What's in a game? Fun, rules and scoring.	
Creative and problem-solving		"Can you compete against yourself, using the elements of the game we have identified and without equipment?"	
Questions and answers	Revising previous week's games in twos.	Two girls demonstrated their game; the competitive element was speed of completion.	
Problem-solving		Pairs each made up a game that included speed of completion as the competitive element (no equipment).	Many pupils found this difficult, but there were some good ideas. (Differentiation must be dealt with next week.)
	Demonstrating two games.	One game involved the elements of speed and timing as the competitive element. The other game involved strength as the competitive element.	I wanted to introduce reciprocal teaching here, but the children wanted to move on in creating their own game.
Guided discovery Problem-solving Creating	Adding an item, in this case a skipping rope (they were not yet ready to make a choice).	"Does this make any difference to your game?" "Can you play a similar game, keeping to the same elements agreed upon?"	It took a long time to calm the children into thinking with their piece of equipment. They were beginning to think up some very good ideas, but time was up. This aspect must be reintroduced next week.

Figure 7.3 Lesson 5

15 October 1986

Strategy	Work covered	Questions and responses	Outcomes
Teacher-directed	Warm-up: on-the-spot shuttles.		Warm-up was very vigorous and tightly structured to include non-verbal instructions — listening, watching and doing.
Questions and answers (revision)	Revision of previous week's elements of game: [see next column]	... fun, rules, scoring (even alone).	These were well remembered.
Guided discovery	Experimenting with a ball.	All the ways the ball can be moved, but keeping it close to your body (also exploring other people's ideas).	Pupils produced many very good ideas, explored them well and tried each other's ideas.
Problem-solving and creative	Making up a game, alone and with a ball.	Game involving fun, rules and scoring.	The games went well: again there were many good ideas. However, two children needed a more restricted programme, as the concentration span was too long for them.

Two groups:

Strategy	Work covered	Questions and responses	Outcomes
● problem-solving	Can your game involve another person?	Pairs each played a game one partner had made up (speed to be introduced later where appropriate).	Pairs did well at this, but most changed their games and started again. We did not move onto the speed aspect, as there was enough already for them to cope with. We did not consider ideas as a class, owing to lack of time.
● guided discovery	Games in twos: [see next column]	● one against one ● with a ball ● area ● scoring points ● fun	The games were not applicable in the end.

Figure 7.4 Lesson 6

5 November 1986

Strategy	Work covered	Questions and responses	Outcomes
Teacher-directed	Warm-up, including footwork		
Creative	Revision: using a ball, keeping it moving and keeping it close (using a foam ball if indoors to provide new experience).	Using various parts of the body, and exploring ideas.	
Brain-storming	Revision: game with a partner.	What does a game involve?	
Problem-solving	Introducing cooperation. Directed and non-directed activities.	"Find an activity that means working with a partner, and explore it." "Now do a specific task: eg bounce the ball to your partner — try to do ten or twenty bounces together; explore this task." "What is the difference between this game and the other game?"	
Problem-solving	Two-against-one game	The two worked together; the one had to try and get the ball, while the other two kept the ball moving. Depending on results, the game might be limited to moving with the hands or feet.	
Problem-solving	Two-against-two game	"What problems did you encounter?" "Was it easier with your hands or your feet?" Relying on earlier results.	
	Aiming towards understanding.	Competition; co-operation; how to cooperate in possession games.	

Figure 7.5 Lesson 9

3 December 1986

Strategy	Work covered	Questions and responses	Outcomes
Teacher-directed	Warm-up.	Using a ball: moving it around a space and keeping it close to various body parts.	Very few chose to work in isolation. The majority opted for cooperation.
Problem-solving and creative Brain-storming	Thinking about the previous week's lesson, and the elements of a game. Cooperation or competition.	A choice of style of game. A choice of equipment: ● large/small ball ● rope ● both. Choice of player combination: ● alone ● in twos ● in threes.	Larger groups were beginning to see how the game consisted of cooperation *and* competition, but so far only a few. Many of the children seemed to find the competitive idea somewhat alien, so maybe there should be greater emphasis placed on cooperative games at this stage.

7.2 Case Study 6

King Alfred's School, Burnham-on-Sea, Somerset
Theme: Invasion Games
Class: 1st Year Secondary
Teacher: Paul Stoddart

Introduction

My part in Somerset's particular project focused upon an invasion-games course which my department operates in the first-year PE programme.

At the time my research for the project began, our invasion-games course was in its second year of operation. Following an evaluation exercise after twelve months, the course had been slightly amended, in that greater detail had been incorporated into the planning of each individual lesson.

The course is taught in the school's sports hall for one lesson per week over a half-term period. The groups are taught in tutor groupings, and each group contains both boys and girls.

The course focuses basically on tactical awareness by helping pupils to learn about the principles of play that are at the core of our approach. Skills are not, therefore, the central aim of this series of lessons, and staff have tried to adopt a "teaching for understanding" approach from the onset of this particular course.

A conscious effort has been made to develop a problem-solving style of teaching for this work. (The appendix includes a detailed rationale for this specific scheme of work, which will give an indication of what my department is trying to achieve in the invasion-games course.)

We had already partly adopted the problem-solving approach, and we felt that the invasion games course would be particularly well suited to meeting Somerset's requirements for the National Study Group project. Also, members of the department had been making determined efforts to incorporate the problem-solving style into this area of the PE programme in particular. This style, therefore, was not alien to me, and I was able to direct more of my preparatory efforts towards the pupils' acquisition of (and participation in) the three "personal" skills which Somerset teachers had planned to isolate and develop in each lesson.

When I sat down to plan each lesson, I soon realised that it would be the personal-skills work which would prove difficult to carry out and monitor. A number of problems presented themselves:

● How could I make sure that each pupil had made a particular decision?

● How could I ensure that pupils were actually listening, either to me or to each other?

● How could the pupils' reflections be assessed?

● How could I create an environment in which they were able to reflect on a past experience?

It was in fact comparatively straightforward for me to plan my normal invasion-games lesson, in which I would concentrate the pupils' thoughts on a theme of tactical awareness and set suitable tasks for them to solve. However, there was now a second barrel on the gun which had to be fired, and the "make a decision — listen — reflect" bullet was certainly going to prove more difficult to load.

Before I embarked upon the actual teaching, my strongest reservations were concerned with striking a suitable compromise between teaching the existing content of the invasion-games course and developing the personal-skills work. It soon became very evident to me that in such situations the teaching process is often at least as important as the actual content of the teaching, if not more important.

Lesson 1
Theme: *"How can we keep possession?"*

Objectives

1. To introduce the pupils to this new six-lesson block of work.

2. To introduce the pupils to one form of a passing-and-handling invasion game.

3. For pupils to be able to recognise and recall a variety of invasion games.

4. For pupils to gain some understanding of the tactics that enable a team to maintain possession of the ball.

5. To assist all pupils in decision-making, listening and reflecting.

Organisation of the invasion game

● A small-team game (preferably teams of three) using a badminton court for the playing area.

● A passing-and-handling game (no running with the ball) so as to develop the pass-and-move technique. Pupils could choose ball type.

● Scoring was by passing to a team-mate who had run into the double lines at the end of the court; he or she had to make a clean catch in order to score a point.

Key points

1. **Tactical solution**
   Hold the ball. Distribute the ball.

2. **Pupil requirements**

   On the ball:

   ● select a receiver (choosing best pass option);

   ● practise deception (disguising the pass);

   ● make a good pass (safety first; possession).

Off the ball:

● create personal space (freeing yourself from defenders);

● identify cues (ie be ready to receive);

● receive the ball (in a good catching position).

3. **Personal skills**

   Decision-making
   Each pupil had to play a part in the rule-making process. This allowed games to run without too much intervention from the teacher. A closed-eyes thinking session was held early on in the lesson in order to implement or amend rules. Each pupil had to express his or her thoughts verbally.

   Listening
   The pupils had to learn to listen properly, both to the teacher and to their class-mates. This was achieved by an ongoing question-and-answer format, and a brainstorming session at the end to elicit class ideas.

   Reflecting
   Pupils had to think about what went well for them, as well as drawing out any unpleasant experiences. They responded verbally to my questions at the very end of the lesson.

Problems posed at appropriate points in the lesson

Q Do we need to modify/alter/change our games in order to make them work better?

R *The pupils suggested changes to the rules.*

Q How can I make some space for myself in order to receive the ball?
A *By dodging away from defenders, and changing the speed and direction.*

Q What sorts of passes are safest?
A *Low, flat, fast passes over short distances.*

Q What sorts of passes are least safe?
A *High, slow lobs over long distances.*

Q How do I choose the best receiver before I actually give the pass?
A *Who is closest to goal, or who is in the best receiving position away from a defender?*

Q Can you tell your partners what your new rule was?
R *Partners listened carefully.*

Q Think about some of the things we've done in the lesson. What went well and what did you enjoy? What didn't go too well that you didn't enjoy much?
R *Pupils reflected on these questions.*

Evaluation

Most pupils seemed to grasp this particular game quite easily. One early problem was that several pupils were holding onto the ball for a long time before passing, not realising this was hindering their attacking progress by giving defenders too much time. I stopped the group and pointed this out.

I found myself torn between concentrating pupils' efforts on the physical/cognitive responses (as I would normally do in an invasion-games block of work) and thinking my way round developing the three chosen personal skills. I was already becoming over-concerned about covering what "we normally do", whereas I should have been more concerned with the personal skills. I felt that these, and the process by which they were to be elicited, would become increasingly important as the weeks progressed. However, I still felt that I should be looking at every opportunity to improve pupils' tactical awareness, just as in a normal invasion-games lesson.

It was my very first session with this group of first-years, and I was pleased with their efforts and thoughtfulness. Many of the boys and the girls gave me the early impression that they were quite able.

I felt that the verbal response method (to my questioning) would not be adequate for the whole block of work. It was very difficult to monitor their responses precisely. (I can only write so fast!) Also some pupils were quieter than others and not so willing to put forward their views.

As I expected, it was evident early on that the pupils were generally not used to solving tasks for themselves in games situations. Perhaps they had been subjected to a good deal of "being told exactly what to do" in their junior schools. Some were slow to warm to the idea of providing some of their own answers and responses to problems.

Examples of pupil responses

1. **Tactical awareness** (Theme: Maintaining possession)

Q What happens if you hold onto the ball?
A *One of their team gets in the way.*

Q Who should I pass to?
A_1 *Someone who is free.*
A_2 *One of my own team*
A_3 *Somebody in the lines if I can.*

Q Which passes are safe? Describe them.
A_1 *Ones which don't go very far.*
A_2 *Flat ones that don't bounce.*

Apart from the questions which I asked, several useful responses were forthcoming in the pupils' actual play. They disguised their passes well, once the idea had been suggested, and they tried hard to find different ways of getting away from their markers.

2. **Decision-making**
During the closed-eyes thinking session I asked everybody to think of a helpful rule. Their answers indicated that about half the group had not been able to think of one. Suggestions included the following:

A_1 *Only one step allowed when you catch the ball.*
A_2 *The catcher is not allowed in all the time.*
A_3 *The same player can't score more than once.*
A_4 *Change the teams so that each has a good player.*
A_5 *You can't knock it out of their hands.*

I wasn't very happy about this particular aspect of the lesson. I had not given sufficient thought to the best way of recording it. It is indeed difficult to ensure that every pupil makes a decision.

3. Listening

I had reminded pupils on several occasions throughout the lesson that they should listen carefully to what was being said, both by me and by other pupils.

My questioning revealed a good level of understanding of how to keep possession of the ball. Most of the lesson's rules were also recalled. However, not every pupil answered a question. Many did, but a few did not.

4. Reflecting

Again, I asked pupils at the very end of the lesson to sit and think back.

Q What had gone well/was enjoyable?
A_1 *Not much arguing.*
A_2 *They gave us the ball back quickly.*
A_3 *He said "sorry" when he knocked me over.*
A_4 *It was a nice game.*

Q What hadn't gone too well/ wasn't enjoyable?
A_1 *When two kept tugging at the ball.*
A_2 *Some people wouldn't move out of their goal lines.*
A_3 *Long passes kept going out.*

I was also very conscious that I probably hadn't involved everyone. Perhaps I had in that they had possibly all reflected for a minute in silence on their own; just because they hadn't answered verbally didn't mean that they hadn't answered in their own minds.

Lesson 2
Theme: "How can we invade the territory?"

Objectives

1. To introduce the pupils to a different form of invasion game.

2. For pupils to become more acquainted with solving problems in the game for themselves.

3. For pupils to appreciate some of the tactics involved in invading the opponent's goal area.

4. For pupils to gain experience in expressing some of their thoughts in questionnaire format.

5. To assist all pupils in decision-making, listening and reflecting.

Organisation of the invasion game

● Teams were slightly larger than in the previous week's game (fives or sixes), and half of the sports hall (ie two badminton courts) was used for the playing area.

● It was a passing game (ie no running with the ball), and pupils chose which ball to use.

● Scoring was by hitting the ball against a cone with a chalk circle (2m diameter) drawn around it.

Key points

1. Tactical solution
Penetrate the defence. Disperse the attack. Support the attack.

2. Pupil requirements

On the ball:

● pass forward (selecting a receiver in front of the ball);

● pass quickly (to avoid delay);

● pass accurately (trying to avoid transposition).

Off the ball:

● take up positions that provide the best support;

● run up the blind side (an element of surprise);

● create space (freeing yourself from defenders).

3. Personal skills

Decision-making
At a suitable point in the game I sat the pupils down and asked them what they thought was the best way to involve all their teammates in the game. They did not answer out loud, but returned to their games and wrote down their answers individually in a questionnaire at the end of the lesson.

Listening
Each pupil had to listen to a selection of their team's answers to the question posed above. The teams were each given a time-out, and ideas were suggested for everyone to listen to. Each team's ideas

were listed in the questionnaire at the end of the lesson.

Reflecting

Each pupil had to reflect on what he or she thought was the best way to involve everyone in the game (giving reasons), and to assess his or her contribution to helping the team invade the opponents' territory.

The questionnaire at the end of the lesson gave pupils time to mull over their experiences of the lesson.

Problems posed at appropriate points in the lesson

Q How can we get the ball into their goal under pressure?
A *Move the ball and players forward.*

Q What sort of passing will help us?
A *Short, quick, accurate passes.*

Q Why might we need to pass quickly?
A *To get into the opponents' territory as quickly as possible.*

Q Where should I go when I haven't got the ball?
A *In front; forwards.*

Q Why?
A *To get to the opponents' end of the court.*

Q How can we make sure everyone is involved in the game?
R *Pupils' own responses were shared afterwards in the team time-out.*

Q How can we stop the defenders from bunching together?

A *Attackers should spread out to try and draw defenders away from goal.*

Evaluation

Pupils made a good start in the game situations. Much seemed to have been remembered from the previous week, in that they got straight back into passing and moving.

The game started to break down as pupils held onto the ball for too long, thus enabling defenders to concentrate around their goals and/or the ball-handler.

I made a conscious effort to get my key point across: pass the ball forwards and support in front of the ball whenever possible. I was particularly pleased with the girls and some of their physical responses to problems set in the game. In general they seemed quicker to grasp the idea of moving forwards as soon as they had passed to a team-mate, and consequently took up some excellent supporting positions.

The idea of running up the blind side was somewhat too advanced at this stage. Although pupils offered some verbal responses to problems on this, they did not put them into practice in the game. The answer offered by pupils of spreading out when attacking was demonstrated very well when they actually played.

Examples of pupil responses

1. **Tactical awareness** (Theme: Invading the territory)

Q If we want to pressurise their goal, what is important about our passing?
A$_1$ *Pass to our players*
A$_2$ *Pass towards their goals.*
A$_3$ *Move the ball forwards.*
A$_4$ *Pass safely.*

Q Where should I try and run to when I haven't got the ball?
A$_1$ *To find a space.*
A$_2$ *In front of our player who is holding the ball.*
A$_3$ *Closer to their goal.*

Q How can we stop the defenders blocking our passes?
A$_1$ *Get rid of the ball quickly.*
A$_2$ *Pass to one of our players as soon as I get it.*

2. **Decision-making**
I asked everyone to sit and think how best to involve all their team-mates in the game. I deliberately did not request answers there and then, as their answers were to be used later in team discussions.

Not being able to read minds, I realised I was unable to monitor the extent to which each child was (or was not) making a decision! Some indication, however, would be given from the answers on the questionnaire.

3. **Listening**
At the time-out stage I asked all pupils to listen carefully to the ideas of other team-mates. I said that they would need to remember some of the ideas to write down later.

As I went from group to group, some interesting thoughts were being expressed.

Examples from questionnaire:

Q What ways did your team suggest for involving all team members in the game?
A_1 *Don't just pass it to your best friend or a good player.*
A_2 *Not passing to only two people.*
A_3 *All our team should have held the ball before shooting at the goal.*
A_4 *Pass to everybody before scoring.*
A_5 *Have the not-so-good people attacking.*
A_6 *When someone has scored, they can't score again till everyone in the team has scored.*

4. **Reflecting**
Written answers at the end of the lesson:

Q What did you do to help your team invade the other team's territory?
A_1 *I did some dummy runs so that the other team's players would mark me and we could score a goal.*
A_2 *I spread out with other players on my team.*
A_3 *I got into a space where I was not being marked.*
A_4 *I made short passes and very occasionally long ones.*
A_5 *I threw to the front.*

I was happier this time with recording some of the pupils' responses in writing. It was not ideal, but it was certainly more solid than the previous week. Much thought was still needed on the wording of the questions.

Lesson 3
Theme: "How can we stop them scoring?"

Objectives

1. To introduce the pupils to basic ideas involved in defensive tactics.

2. For pupils to become familiar with person-to-person and zone defensive systems.

3. To develop a method of completing questionnaires as a means of evaluation.

4. To assist all pupils in decision-making, listening and reflecting.

Organisation of the invasion game

- Teams were in fives where possible, and the court area occupied half the sports hall, using the cross-court basketball area.

- It was a passing game (ie no running with the ball), and pupils had a choice of ball.

- Scoring was shooting through the basketball rings in the normal way.

- Person-to-person defence came first, and then zone defence.

Key points

1. **Tactical solution**
Deny shooting space. Defend the target.

2. **Pupil requirements**

On the ball:

- mark the goal side (make sure you know what that means);

- block the striker (prevent him from trying to shoot);

- block the ball-handler (prevent a forward pass).

Off the ball:

- stay on the goal side (the correct position for marking a running opponent);

- person-to-person defence (marking one player each);

- zone defence (marking space, not players).

3. **Personal skills**

Decision-making
Each pupil had to decide which defensive system he or she preferred (person-to-person or zone), and give reasons why. Pupils were given experience of both systems, and wrote their answers down in the questionnaire.

Listening
Each pupil had to think of the possible advantages and disadvantages of one particular defence system. They formed pairs, and one partner gave his answer to the other, who had to listen carefully. The listener repeated the answer back to the original teller, who then gave the listener a rating (good–bad) on the questionnaire. Pupils also had to write out a list of things to remember about the two systems.

Reflecting
Pupils had to think back to what they enjoyed (if anything!) about the lesson, and to say which system they preferred. Written

answers were given in the questionnaire at the end of the lesson.

Problems posed at appropriate points in the lesson

Q Who is the most dangerous player?
A *The one with the ball.*

Q Who shall I mark?
A *The closest person to me.*

Q If I don't mark a player, what else is there to mark?
A *A space or zone.*

Q What is the best place to stand when I'm marking someone?
A *The goal side — ie between opponent and goal.*

Q What can I do to put off the passer?
A *Wave my arms in front to stop him passing forwards.*

Q When you're zoning, what's the first thing to do when they regain possession?
A *Run back and set up your defence.*

Evaluation

It soon became obvious in the early stages that it would be most unwise for me to attempt to cover both methods of defending in the one lesson. It would mean merely scratching the surface of both, and getting no real depth of learning. I therefore decided to concentrate this particular lesson just on the person-to-person system.

Pupils soon tuned into looking for someone to mark when transposition occurred. Inevitably some defenders would mark the same person, so I stressed that sometimes someone would have to run and mark the attacker who had broken away quickly down-court.

One problem of this game was that pupils often threw away possession in the early stages of the game by throwing up shots from too far out. This was not too bad a thing to happen in one respect, as it meant that both games involved instances of an attack that turned into a defence.

Throughout this particular lesson I felt happier in myself about trying to achieve a balance between the physical content of the lesson and the development of personal skills. I was a little happier about my method of monitoring pupil responses than in the first lesson, and felt that I was becoming accustomed to incorporating the personal and physical components into one lesson. I was gradually devoting an increasing amount of time to the three personal skills, which were becoming my main priority in the lesson.

Examples of pupil responses

1. **Tactical awareness** (Theme: Prevention of scoring)

   Q Who is the most important person to mark?
   A_1 *Their best player.*
   A_2 *The person with the ball.*
   A_3 *The passer.*

   Q What can we do to stop them scoring?
   A_1 *Put our hands up in front of the player holding the ball.*
   A_2 *Crowd round the ball.*
   A_3 *Block the ball.*

   Q What could we do as a team in defence?
   A_1 *Each mark a player and follow him.*
   A_2 *Crowd around the goal to stop them.*
   A_3 *Try and intercept their passes.*
   A_4 *All of our team have to work hard.*

There were also some excellent physical responses to the problems posed in pupils' game play, indicating a certain degree of cognitive development on the part of many pupils.

2. **Decision-making**
   This aspect of the personal skills fell by the wayside on this occasion. Pupils could not make an informed decision as to their preferred defensive system, because we were concentrating on person-to-person defending. This decision would have to be deferred until next week, when we would be dealing with zone defence. Pupils would hopefully be able to recall some of today's experiences and findings.

   I had originally thought it feasible to deal with both systems, but in my planning I had not taken into account the chunk of time in these lessons which is needed for the development of personal skills.

3. **Listening**
   The group worked in pairs. The amendment to the original lesson plan meant that pupils were unable to compare the systems. So instead I asked them to think of the advantages and disadvantages

of person-to-person defending and repeat them to listening partners.

One partner concentrated on listening, and repeated his partner's answer. On the questionnaire the listener was given a rating by the teller.

When pupils listed as many things as they could remember, this highlighted many principal points. Here are some examples:

A_1 *Keep in front of them.*
A_2 *Mark the other team.*
A_3 *Try to stop the ball.*
A_4 *Do not let him pass.*
A_5 *Wherever she/he goes, you follow.*
A_6 *No more than one person should mark each player.*
A_7 *When a player goes to shoot, put your hands in front so he/she can't score.*
A_8 *Guard someone with your hands in the air.*
A_9 *Keep looking out of the corner of your eye at the person you're marking.*
A_{10} *If they start to dodge, stay with them.*
A_{11} *Try and intercept the ball.*

Many more excellent points were remembered.

4. **Reflecting**
A number of reflections were recorded at the very end of the lesson:

Q What did you most enjoy about today's lesson?
A_1 *Coming to PE.*
A_2 *The game, because when we scored they didn't argue and vice versa.*

A_3 *Playing with all of my friends.*
A_4 *I most enjoyed shooting at goal for our team.*
A_5 *Winning the game.*
A_6 *I like working as a team.*
A_7 *That you get the ball a lot of times.*
A_8 *Scoring a goal, having fun, running about.*

Q Why do we need to listen to others?
A_1 *Because you might not hear an instruction.*
A_2 *You might miss something.*
A_3 *For example, if your mother said "Look before you cross the road" and you didn't, you could well get run over.*
A_4 *We need to listen to understand.*
A_5 *We can learn from them.*
A_6 *Because they might be saying something very important.*
A_7 *They have other ideas to make the game go better.*

Lesson 4
Theme: "How can we stop them scoring?"

Objectives

1. To reinforce some basic principles of defending.

2. For pupils to be able to differentiate between the person-to-person and zone systems of defence.

3. To highlight the main ways of setting up a zone defence around a basket.

4. To assist all pupils in decision-making, listening and reflecting.

Organisation of the invasion game

● Teams of five where possible to make two games of five-versus-five, using the same playing area as the previous week — half the sports hall for each cross-court game.

● A passing game (no running with the ball), with the pupils choosing the type of ball.

● Scoring by shooting into the basketball rings.

● A brief recap of the person-to-person system, with the bulk of the lesson on zoning.

Key points

1. **Tactical solution**
Deny shooting space. Defend target area.

2. **Pupil requirements**

On the ball:

● mark a player when he or she is in your space;

● block a shot or pass (work hard to discourage the ball-handler).

Off the ball:

● maintain the shape of the defence (don't be drawn out of position);

● present a unified barrier (eg all waving your arms);

● mark your space (don't follow off-ball players).

3. Personal skills

Decision-making

Each pupil had to decide on a preferred system of defence, and give reasons. Pupils had experienced both systems, and wrote their answers in the questionnaire.

Each team also had to decide on a method of setting up their zone around the basket. Pupils were given time to go back and discuss this and sort out a formation.

Listening

Each pupil was asked to listen carefully for important points about zone defence. Teams were given a time-out to decide what things defenders can do once they are in the zone. They responded verbally and gave a written summary on the sheet at the end of the lesson.

Reflecting

Each pupil had to decide which of the two methods of defending they preferred, with reasons. Written answers were to be given in the questionnaire at the end of the lesson.

Problems posed at appropriate points in the lesson

Q What do I mark in a zone defence?
A *A space or an area of the court.*

Q What should my team do when the opposition regains possession?
A *Run back towards our goal area and set up the defence.*

Q Who marks the person with the ball?

A *The defender in whose area the ball-handler happens to be.*

Q What does goal side mean?
A *The area between the attacker and my goal.*

Q Can teams go away to their own basket for a couple of minutes, and discuss what sort of zone they might set up?
R *Teams reponded with an actual demonstration.*

Q How can we put the other team off when they are attacking us?
A *Present a barrier of arms.*

Evaluation

As a warm-up and introduction to the lesson, I set up a game similar to the previous week's, using person-to-person defence. The group were able to recall many of the key factors for this type of defence.

This particular group was starting to impress me a great deal, not only by the pupils' generally favourable attitude towards this series of lessons, but also with their excellent responses to the problems which I set throughout the lessons. They were really quite "switched on", and I was becoming convinced, more than ever before, of the positive effects on cognitive development which a problem-solving approach might have. Many if not all of the pupils were producing good responses, and acquiring knowledge and understanding about some of the tactics involved, albeit at a low level, in the games they played. As the group was a complete tutor-group, it was of very mixed ability, and I was confident that pupils of all abilities were benefitting from this sort of work.

When we started work on the zone defence, both of the games broke down regularly in their early stages because the defending team did not retreat to their own basket area when transposition occurred. This had the undesirable effect of causing the attackers to rush their offence, and they often threw the ball away. I therefore had to put a condition on the game that defenders had to retreat behind a certain line as soon as their offence had broken down.

I was making conscious efforts to give the pupils the opportunity of solving the set problems for themselves, without too much intervention from me. I was constantly trying to word my questions properly to leave them fairly open-ended for pupil interpretation. Questions that were not worded appropriately might push the pupils towards the outcome preferred by the teacher. It is all to do with that thin line that divides problem-solving from guided discovery.

Examples of pupil responses

1. **Tactical awareness** (Theme: Prevention of scoring — zone defence)

Q If I don't mark a player, what else could I mark?
A_1 *A place on the court.*
A_2 *A space.*
A_3 *The goal.*
A_4 *The basket.*

Q When the ball comes into my space, what should I do?
A_1 *Stop the player scoring.*
A_2 *Try and get it.*
A_3 *Intercept it.*
A_4 *Block a pass or a shot.*

Q How can we put the other team off?
A₁ Put our hands in the air.
A₂ All put our hands up.
A₃ Wave our arms fast.

Q What sort of zone can you set up?

Team answers

The following were demonstrated to the other three teams:

TEAM 1:

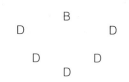

A half-circle barrier around the basket.

TEAM 2:

Four in a semi-circle barrier; one person free to chase the ball.

TEAM 3:

One tall player under the basket; four in a straight line in front.

TEAM 4:

```
              B

      D   D   D

      D   D   D
```

Two rows with three in each.

Key: B = Basket
       D = Defender

2. **Decision-making**
The pupils had to decide which method of defending they preferred and why. The decision was a reasonably straightforward one, and the reasons given provided an insight into how much they had understood of the principles. Some examples are given in section 4 below.

Additionally, each team was asked to set up their own zone formation. Quite a lot of discussion took place before a final team decision was arrived at, and the results are shown diagramatically above.

3. **Listening**
During a time-out, defender teams discussed what they could usefully do when defending their zones. Each pupil needed to listen, and later wrote down his or her answers individually on the questionnaire. Here are some examples of answers given:

A₁ Get back to your goal when they get the ball.
A₂ Be ready for the ball.
A₃ Mark a space around the goal area.
A₄ Wave our hands about.

A₅ Get the ball when it hits the goal.
A₆ Space out.
A₇ Form a semi-circle around the goal.
A₈ Gather round the goal.
A₉ Bend over the person who is shooting.

4. **Reflecting**
Pupils decided on their preferred system, giving their reasons:

Zone
A₁ I can see where the ball is.
A₂ Everyone is round the goal and it makes it harder for the person who is shooting.
A₃ It is a lot easier, and there is not so much running.
A₄ It makes a better game.

Person-to-person
A₅ It is more interesting than marking a space.
A₆ You have to lose your marker.
A₇ I like dodging around.
A₈ Everyone has something to do.
A₉ It gives you a chance to stay in the game, and you don't have to run back to the goal when the other team gets the ball.

Lesson 5
Theme: "How can we score?"

Objectives

1. For pupils to experience a new type of invasion game: running with the ball.

2. For pupils to be able to differentiate between a lineball and a goal game.

3. For pupils to gain some understanding of the tactics involved in the scoring of goals/points.

4. To assist all pupils in decision-making, listening and reflecting.

Organisation of the invasion game

● Using the entire sports hall for a game of lineball — ie rugby-style (widthways).

● A try to be scored by touching down in the normal way, along the length of the sports hall.

● The first game in which pupils had the opportunity to run/travel with the ball. Touch tackles.

● Class divided into two teams (if too many on the day using substitutes for umpires etc).

Key points

1. **Tactical solution**
   Create a shooting space. Attack the target.

2. **Pupil requirements**

   On the ball:

   ● take on a defender (try and beat the opponent);

   ● create one-to-ones (encourage a player to take on a defender);

   ● shoot/score (take responsibility).

   Off the ball:

   ● tempt a defender from the target (run off the ball);

   ● spread defenders out (to create gap to run through);

● provide support (help each other to pass to the back or side to create spaces [outlet pass]).

3. **Personal skills**

Decision-making
Each pupil had to decide upon a rule to make this game more difficult to play, and write it down in the questionnaire at the end.

Listening
Each pupil had to listen carefully to the discussion of attacking principles, giving priority to what you should do when you receive the ball. They then wrote their response in the questionnaire.

Additionally, pupils had to decide in pairs (talking and listening) on the best way for attackers to make the defenders spread out.

Reflecting
Each pupil had to think about the major differences between today's invasion game and all the previous games. Their conclusions were to be written down in the questionnaire at the end of the lesson.

Problems posed at appropriate points in the lesson

Q What is meant by taking on a defender?
A *Trying to beat him; running past him.*

Q What should I be looking to do first when I get the ball?
A *Run through the defence.*

Q How could we stop the defenders from bunching together?

A *Spread the attackers out; we have a long goal line to score on, so there should be spaces.*

Q What is the best direction to run with the ball?
A *Forwards if possible.*

Q Decide in pairs how we could get the defenders widely dispersed.
R *Listen to your partner, then explain how to disperse the attackers.*

Q If I'm running with the ball, when should I pass it on?
A *If you can't go all the way and score, or if a defender comes in towards you, draw the defender, then pass the ball on.*

Evaluation

This was possibly the best lesson of the block so far. The pupils worked extremely well, and boys and girls alike took to the lineball game immediately.

As expected, it took a few minutes before they were used to the idea of running with the ball in their hands (this was the first game where it had been allowed). Also many pupils to start with took too long before passing on the ball when they had been touch-tackled. However, once these minor hiccoughs had been ironed out, the game flowed.

The group warmed to a game with larger teams, although I was apprehensive about plunging them into a game with teams of nine. They spread out well, and seemed to have retained some of the comments we had made about dispersal, which they put to good practice in the main.

The group had decided to play with a size-4 mouldmaster rugby ball — not the first time pupils had chosen to handle this shape of ball; so many had had previous opportunities to become familiar with the awkward shape.

I was very pleased to see individual boys and girls alike taking responsibility for running with the ball as a first priority when they gained possession. This point did not need too much labouring.

I could definitely see now that pupils were much happier to solve some of the problems for themselves in the game situations. In the first lesson I had noticed clearly how they were used to being told to do a good deal by their teacher. It was evident that they had developed since then. Now, instead of being taught, they spent more time learning for themselves.

Examples of pupil responses

1. **Tactical awareness**
   (Theme: How can we score?)

   Q What do we mean by taking on a defender?
   A_1 Trying to beat him.
   A_2 Getting past them.
   A_3 Going away from him and trying to score.

   Q What is the best direction to run with the ball?
   A_1 To score.
   A_2 Forwards: you could get through and score.
   A_3 Towards the opposite goal.
   A_4 Away from the defenders.

2. **Decision-making**
   The pupils were asked to work out a rule which could have been implemented to make the game more difficult to play.

   A_1 You have to pass to five people in your team before scoring.
   A_2 Using the sports hall the other way round, ie lengthways instead of crossways.
   A_3 You can only have one person that can score.
   A_4 You are only allowed to score once each.

   A good percentage of the class gave one or more of these salient responses.

3. **Listening**
   First the pupils were asked what they should do first upon receiving the ball. Here are some examples of their written answers:

   A_1 Run to a space.
   A_2 Run towards goal.
   A_3 Run towards a space and pass if tagged.
   A_4 See if there is a space to run into, and if so run into it.
   A_5 Run with it and look for a space to run into.
   A_6 You should run for the line.

   Secondly they were asked to talk in pairs and listen to their partner, afterwards reversing roles, to decide on the best way to disperse defenders. Here are some examples of verbal responses:

   A_1 Our team should spread out so that they follow us.
   A_2 Use the wide parts of the court.

   A_3 Run down the sides of the pitch.
   A_4 Our team shouldn't crowd together, otherwise we're easy to tag.
   A_5 We shouldn't get too close to our own team.

   These answers were also translated well into practice, as both teams made good use of the spaces (thus dispersing the defence) throughout the lesson.

4. **Reflecting**
   The class was asked to think back over previous lessons, and make comparisons between them and this lesson (it was the first time they had been allowed to carry the ball). Here are some examples of their responses:

   A_1 We had to touch the floor with the ball to score.
   A_2 We had further to run; only two teams with more players.
   A_3 We were attacking a line; we could run with the ball; we were allowed to make contact; we had more space to attack and play.
   A_4 We had a bigger area to play in.
   A_5 How you move.
   A_6 This time you had to be tagged to stop, but in the other games you had to stop as soon as you got the ball.
   A_7 We were running with the ball.

Lesson 6
Theme: "How do we regain possession?"

Objectives

1. For pupils to gain some understanding of the tactics involved in winning back the ball.

2. For pupils to recognise the importance of setting up their defence quickly when transposition occurs.

3. To differentiate between intercepting and tackling.

4. To assist all pupils in decision-making, listening and reflecting.

5. To encourage pupils to make a physical challenge for the ball.

Organisation of the invasion game

- Teams of five as near as possible, with a court area of half the sports hall.

- A passing-and-moving game (no carrying of the ball).

- Scoring by shooting the ball through the basketball rings.

- Pupils were allowed to choose the type of ball.

Key points

1. **Tactical solution**
   Dispossess the attack.

2. **Pupil requirements**

   On the ball:

   - tackle the ball-handler (knock the ball out of his hands);

   - intercept (be alert in reading the pass; block the ball from prying hands).

   Off the ball:

   - maintain your positions (maintain the shape of the defence);

   - anticipate the pass (try to catch the ball before it reaches a receiver);

   - anticipate a transposition (try and "tempt" the pass and steal it).

3. **Personal skills**

Decision-making
Each pupil had to decide on ways of regaining possession, and to give a written response in the questionnaire.

Listening
Each member of the class was encouraged to listen to various strategies for regaining possession of the ball, and to give a written response in the questionnaire.

Each pupil also had to give a written definition of the term *intercept*.

Reflecting
Pupils were asked to consider their own feelings when they lost possession of the ball to the other team, and how they felt whenever they personally managed to get the ball back. Both of these responses were to be recorded in the questionnaire at the end of the lesson.

Problems posed at appropriate points in the lesson

Q What is meant by *tackle*?
A *To go in and challenge for the ball, such as by knocking the ball legally from the possessor's hands (eg as in basketball).*

Q What is meant by *intercept*?
A *To get possession of the ball by anticipating a pass before it reaches its intended target.*

Q What should I do when I'm marking the person with the ball?
A *Block them with my hands; try for a steal; block a forward pass or shot; keep to the goal side.*

Q How can my team get the ball back?
A *Tackle (ie knock the ball out of the possessor's hands) or intercept.*

Q What should you do as soon as you lose the ball?
A *Quickly set up your defence; be alert; be aggressive in trying to win the ball back.*

Evaluation

This was the final lesson in the block of six. It also turned out to be the lesson that very nearly wasn't! In my initial long-term planning I had overlooked the fact that the final lesson of the block was going to clash with the school's annual fund-raising sponsored walk. Thus six lessons were unexpectedly reduced to five.

However, when I explained this fact to the group at the end of Lesson 5, they made several spontaneous suggestions as to ways of fitting in the sixth lesson. Much to my surprise and delight, most of the group was able to come during a lunch hour in order to complete the work. This undoubtedly says something about what they had got out of the course!

The games themselves went very well. The pupils responded enthusiastically to the fact that for the first time they were allowed to dispossess the attackers by physically knocking the ball out of their hands so long as there was no actual body contact.

Just as when introducing the game of basketball, it is well-nigh impossible to stop body contact altogether. The sheer eagerness of the pupils to dispossess attackers leads to some inevitable body contact. Making allowances for this, the pupils made several good steals.

After six lessons I was becoming increasingly confident at helping the pupils to acquire the three desired personal skills, and monitoring the extent to which success had been achieved in each lesson. I had been gradually making a more conscious effort not to dwell on the physical aspects of the lesson content, and to become more concerned with eliciting the personal skills and working on the actual process by which they were being developed.

Examples of pupil responses

1. **Tactical awareness** (Theme: Regaining possession)

   Q What do I mean by tackle?
   A_1 Knocking the ball out of their hands.
   A_2 Getting the ball.
   A_3 Challenging and winning the ball.

   A_4 Going in and getting back the ball.

   Q What should I be doing when I'm marking the person with the ball?
   A_1 Trying to block the ball.
   A_2 Tackling to get it back.
   A_3 Knocking it out of their hands.
   A_4 Not letting them score or make a pass.

2. **Decision-making**
   Pupils were asked to decide on ways in which their team could regain possession of the ball.

   A_1 Snatch.
   A_2 Intercept.
   A_3 Tackle.
   A_4 Hit the ball out of their hands.

   In retrospect I think I limited their written responses somewhat by only giving enough space on the questionnaire for a one- or two-word answer.

3. **Listening**
   I wanted pupils to listen carefully to various strategies which could be adopted to regain possession.

   The first question on the questionnaire went part-way towards answering the previous point (decision-making) as well as this one. Therefore the answers to point 2 above can be used to refer to listening as well.

   Each pupil was also asked to say what they understood by the word intercept.

   A_1 When there's a ball coming and you jump and catch it.

   A_2 You need to catch it when they throw it to one of their players.
   A_3 Block or catch a ball from another person (not on your team) when it was meant for someone on their team.
   A_4 If someone passed to a team-mate, one of the other team could catch it just in front of the person.
   A_5 If someone is going to get the ball you catch it just before the person gets it.
   A_6 Getting the ball before they do when one of their team-mates throws it to them.

4. **Reflecting**
   Pupils were asked to express their feelings about when their team lost possession and when they personally managed to get the ball back.

   Q How did you feel when the opposition won back the ball from your team?
   A_1 Just agreed that it was a fair interception.
   A_2 Determined to get it back.
   A_3 Frustrated, disappointed.
   A_4 I felt angry and I felt guilty if they got the ball off me.
   A_5 I felt we had to get it back fast.

   Q How did you feel when you made an interception, or tackled, or won the ball?
   A_1 Good to get it back.
   A_2 Happy and pleased.
   A_3 Nothing, I concentrated.
   A_4 I had a funny feeling which is hard to explain.
   A_5 Happy that we had another chance of scoring.
   A_6 I felt glad I'd got the ball back.
   A_7 It was great fun and the person didn't complain.

Final Overall Evaluation

It was only when tying up the loose ends after all the teaching had been done, and collating all the information for writing up, that I really began to see some of the ways in which this project had succeeded.

My early apprehensions were to a certain extent borne out at various stages during the block of six lessons. But as the lessons progressed, I felt increasingly more at ease with my task, and better able to concentrate on developing the personal skills as well as carrying out the work of the original scheme.

It is difficult to say in strict terms how accurately I managed to adhere to the problem-solving approach. It can become so awkward for the teacher not to give too much away to pupils and so direct them towards the desired responses. Great care is needed if one is not to stray into a guided-discovery approach. If the set task is left open-ended, this obviously gives pupils a great deal of scope for interpreting and responding to the problem in their own individual ways.

I did in fact feel reasonably at ease with my chosen approach, as I had already taught several blocks of invasion-games work using a problem-solving approach (see Appendix 1). However, I still asked myself frequently whether my method really complied with what was expected in the strategy of problem-solving.

A great many of the pupil responses indicated to me that there was indeed some development in the cognitive aspects of their education. The lesson evaluations, and in particular the pupil responses, demonstrated a good understanding of the work involved. I could quote dozens of responses which bear this out. I would hasten to add that I chose responses from the whole cross-section of the group. The answers cited are not only from the better games-players, or from the more intelligent among this mixed-ability, mixed-sex group. The answers were truly representative of the whole class.

I feel that my teaching has genuinely benefited from my participation in the project. I knew that I had to stand back in certain situations, and not merely provide all the right answers. I certainly had to assist pupils by structuring the right sort of environment where learning could take place, and where suitable responses to set tasks could be sought. Occasionally I was guilty of diving in and doing it for them, but practice makes perfect, given time.

It was reasonably easy to make sure that all pupils were physically active and playing the chosen game. However, my comments after the first lesson highlighted my problems in ensuring that all pupils attempted to find a solution to the tasks.

The development of the three personal skills posed a separate problem. As the weeks progressed, I found myself concentrating more on this than on the original purposes of the invasion-games scheme of work, which at times became almost incidental. I was not too concerned with this, as I recognised the need to try and meet the project's objectives of developing the personal skills. The extent to which these were actually being developed was difficult to monitor, and I decided to use a written record of responses to assist me in this. This also encouraged the listening aspect of the lesson, as pupils knew they would be writing something at the end of the session.

It is probably taken for granted that pupils listen to teachers. It was reassuring for me to encourage the pupils to listen harder, and their answers throughout the lesson indicated that they were certainly doing so. This in itself proved to be an extremely worthwhile exercise.

While the games were being played, there was an abundance of variety in pupils' responses. They were evidently working hard to sort out the various tactical problems in the games, and their solutions were often employed in the decision-making aspect of the lesson.

As expected, I found that the lesson had to be carefully thought out in advance. Even the best planning sometimes goes haywire, as I found when I planned the defending session, and only got through half of the material in the one lesson!

I certainly enjoyed participating in the project, and the pupils' own enjoyment was evident when they asked to complete the final session in their own time out of school hours. This convinced me that at least they had enjoyed the work.

Also, I never failed to be astonished at the pupils' responses to the problems. A great many of their answers were absolutely superb, and this reinforced my conviction that cognitive development was taking place, hopefully on the part of all of the youngsters. Their responses showed an understanding of the games far beyond that which I thought they were capable of, and it was not just the better able who provided good, sound responses.

Finally, I shall submit a detailed report to my department on the findings of the project, both in general and in specific terms. It will then be necessary for us to decide whether we are able to use this sort of work and approach to good effect in our particular school situation.

Appendix 1: Scheme of Work for Invasion Games

The rationale for using an "understanding" approach to teaching

This scheme of work should be taught using a "teaching for understanding" method, as opposed to one which might be skill- or technique-orientated. The emphasis is on a tactical approach to games teaching. It is the principles of play which are at the core of this approach, and these should focus on either attacking or defending principles, depending on which team has possession. The teacher may at some stage consider it beneficial to teach various techniques to pupils, but they should rarely be the central aim of the lesson.

Such a course is intended to help pupils transferring from junior schools to acquire some understanding and knowledge of games, by teaching the "why" before teaching the "how". It is hoped that pupils will gain experience in a variety of invasion games — ie those games in which territories or goals are invaded, such as hockey, soccer, rugby, netball, basketball, handball — as all of these have many points in common as far as tactical awareness is concerned. However, certain invented games may also be added to these, as well as games specially created to develop a certain theme from the block of work. Captain Ball, for example, will help in teaching elementary tactics before the introduction of basketball or netball proper.

Games should be structured so that every member of the group may participate. The rules which determine the game form should be simple enough for everyone to understand. This might lead to a situation where the same game is carried on in various forms within a single lesson in order to suit the needs of various pupils.

Games-playing is very much concerned with making decisions in order to solve certain problems as they arise during the game. A teaching-for-understanding approach should encourage pupils to identify such problems and allow them to consider suitable tactical solutions.

The children should be given some responsibility during the lesson for both the problem-solving and the decision-making aspects of their cognitive processes. This might well mean, therefore, that the teacher carefully points pupils in the right direction and acts as an enabler rather than as a provider of information, which often makes pupils too dependent on the teacher. A considerable onus is placed on the pupils to become involved in their own learning.

Appendix 2: Questionnaires Used in the Project

Lesson 2: How can we invade the territory?

HOW WELL DID I LISTEN?

1. What ways did your team suggest for involving all team members in the game?

2. What sort of things could your team do to help it to invade the opponent's goal?

LOOKING BACK ON MY LESSON!

1. Which way did *you* think was best to get all of your team-mates involved in your game?

2. Why?

3. What did you do to help your team invade the other team's territory?

Lesson 3: How can we stop them scoring?

LISTENING

1. When your partner had to repeat back to you what you had said, he/she was:

☐ EXCELLENT
☐ QUITE GOOD
☐ NOT VERY GOOD
☐ TERRIBLE

2. Choose *either* **Zone** defence *or* **Person-to-person** defence and list as many things as you can remember about it (Number ...)

REFLECTING

1. What did you most *enjoy* about today's lesson?

2. What system do you like best?

☐ ZONE
☐ PERSON-TO-PERSON

3. Why?

4. Why do we need to listen to others?

Lesson 4: How can we stop them scoring?

LISTENING

1. What do I mark with a *zone* defence?

2. What do we need to do in a zone?

    i
    ii
    iii
    iv

REFLECTING

1. Over the last two lessons, which system (**zone** or **person-to-person**) did you like best?

2. Why?

3. Name something enjoyable (if anything!) about today's lesson.

Lesson 5: How can we score?

DECISION

What rules could we have made to make our passing game more difficult?

1.

2.

LISTENING

What is the first thing I should do as an attacker when I have caught a pass from a team-mate?

REFLECTING

1. What did you enjoy about our line-ball game?

2. What were the differences between today's invasion game and all the others we've played?

    i
    ii
    iii
    iv

Lesson 6: How can we regain possession?

LISTENING

1. To get the ball back, my team mates could:

(a) _____ or (b) _____

2. What does *intercept* mean?

REFLECTING

1. How did *you* feel when the opposition won back the ball from your team?

2. How did *you* feel when you made an interception or tackled and won the ball?

3. What was enjoyable about today's lesson?

PART III

OUTCOME

"Specific technical skills were taught in some lessons, and I think there is still a need to do this. The relevant point is surely what and how much is done, and how it is done."

"Decision-making improved when the children had more responsibility."

"Reflection is important. It helped the children to think and clarify the important factors examined within the lesson."

The general focus of the project has been on good practice in the teaching process, with an emphasis on teaching styles and the strategies needed within those styles.

The model created by Philip Waterhouse (*What constitutes good practice and how do we recognise it?*) indicates the areas which relate to good practice in PE teaching. These areas are shown in adapted form below in order to clarify this general focus.

8.1 Areas to Consider when Encouraging Good Practice

1. The environment:
   - how displays are mounted;
   - the arrangement of equipment;
   - cleanliness in the changing rooms;
   - the maintenance of large and small items of PE equipment.

2. The organisation of equipment:
   - where it is stored;
   - how it is collected and put away;
   - the safety element;
   - ease of access during activity.

3. Pupil participation:
   - in the changing area;
   - activity during the lesson;
   - when changing for the activity.

4. Pupil motivation during the lesson.

5. The appropriate use of a range of teaching styles.

6. Class organisation:
   - the development of individuals
   - small groups;
   - whole-class activity.

7. Teacher–pupil and pupil–pupil relationships in a range of physical activities.

8. The appropriateness of the setting, and of a range of physical and intellectual tasks; the challenge extended to the pupil by the teacher, and between one pupil and another.

9. The ability to stop and start the group in a controlled and ordered manner.

10. Evidence of the teacher's planning, preparation and record-keeping.

11. Evidence of methods of observation; feedback from the pupils during and after the lesson.

The central concern of this project has been to develop the teacher's awareness in the selection of appropriate strategies to enhance the learning process through physical education (see point 5 above).

The pages which follow present a series of observation schedules used by different schools and authorities. They can be used in at least two ways:

1. As a checklist to help you reflect on your own teaching (in this case detailed tallying of frequencies is probably unrealistic, but you should try to record the balance achieved between giving instructions, asking questions and setting problems).

2. With the cooperation of a supportive colleague, whom you could invite to observe a lesson.

Observations could focus, either on particular selected criteria that have been agreed on beforehand, or on the schedule as a whole. If criteria are selected, they should be appropriate to the purpose of the lesson.

You could develop your own checklists to focus on any other areas of good practice, such as teacher–pupil and pupil–pupil relationships in a range of physical activities (see point 7 on page 79).

Figure 8.1 Observation Schedule

Class: Activity: Teacher:

Purpose of lesson:

Expected outcomes:

Focus of observation	Tally/recording	Comments	Post-lesson reflection
Note the number of instructions given by the teacher to the class or a group. Has this strategy been over- or under-used for the purposes of the lesson?			*Observer*: Were there any significant interventions on the part of the teacher? Select one to discuss.
Note the number of questions asked which required a specific (ie "correct") answer. Has this strategy been over- or under-used?			
Note the number of problems set to which the pupils might devise a range of responses. Has this strategy been over- or under-used?			
Was sufficient time allowed for thought before the teacher called for (or gave) a response?	yes/no		*Teacher*: Were your selected strategies appropriate to your purpose?
What use did the teacher make of pupils' responses?	● demonstrated/ implemented ● commented on ● ignored		
When were the pupils involved in decision-making?			
Was the organisation of pupil groups appropriate and efficient?			
Were groups clear about their purpose? — ie did they work purposefully without the teacher?			*Agreed*: Action for development.
Were the pupils adequately prepared for the physical challenge of the lesson?			
Was the physical challenge appropriate to the range of abilities within the class?			
Did the pupils seem to be clear as to the purpose of the lesson?			

Figure 8.2 Observer/teacher observation sheet (Rotherham LEA)

Mosston's Spectrum of Teaching Styles

A. Command
B. Practice
C. Reciprocal
D. Self-check
E. Inclusion
F. Guided discovery
G. Problem-solving (divergent)
H. Individual programme (student design)

Organisation:
Teacher:
Class/age:
Activity:

1. Focus of lesson:

2. Resources:

3. Checklist of styles used:

	A	B	C	D	E	F	G	H
generally								
highlighted								
predominant style								

4. Pupil feedback:
   ● group response:
   ● two individuals:

5. Note relationships:
   ● pupil–staff:
   ● pupil–pupil:
   ● staff–pupil:
   ● staff–staff:

6. Comment on achievement of objectives:

7. Brief evaluation:

8.2 Feedback

A key requirement of any teaching/learning strategy is to obtain feedback:

● It helps the teacher to plan.

● It helps the pupil to feel valued.

● It enables the teacher to check the pupils' level of understanding.

How do *you* obtain feedback?

● from observing your classes while you teach?

● through informal questions and discussion with your pupils?

● from questionnaires?

● from pupil self-evaluation?

Examples of Feedback Techniques

A variety of feedback techniques were used by teachers on the projects. The pages which follow include a few sample questionnaires given to pupils or to both teacher and pupils. They were used for obtaining feedback in order to assess how much of the lesson had been understood. Some of the ideas may be helpful to other teachers. (Pupil responses are indicated in italic type.)

Example 1 Redbridge LEA

Teacher: Judith Rock
Class: 1st and 2nd Years
Activity: Gymnastics
Time: Partner-work
Teaching style: G. Problem-solving

Sheet given to pupils in lesson 2 (of 7).

Pupils working in pairs.

Name of pair observing: *Lesley and Samantha*

Name of pair being observed: *Simone and Joann*

Examples of partner-work seen:

over
support moving
under
at the same time
balance support
cannon

What activities were used to show these types of partner work?

cartwheel over
leapfrog
going under a crab
backwards roll
standing on legs
Arab spring

Example 2 Surrey LEA

Teacher: Alison Vinai
Class: 3rd Years
Activity: Volleyball
Teaching style: C. Reciprocal

Review sheets completed at the end of the course (6 weeks), but lesson-by-lesson review may be preferable. At each lesson a new task sheet was given to the pupils. (Lesson 1 only is used as an example.)

Name: *Graham*   Form: *3P*

Look at the task sheet (see overleaf) to remind yourself of the game form, and then complete this sheet.

1. Explain the task set:

   The task was to play a throw-catch game without letting the ball touch the ground. You are allowed two passes and then it must go over the net. The ball may not be struck. If you ground the ball on the opponents' court you score a point. Each game is up to 5 points.

2. What basic tactics and team-play did we develop to make this game work and to achieve our objective?

   The tactics and team-play learned were moving and position, and building an attack. You needed to be at the net with another person and confuse the opposition by making it look as though your partner was about to hit the ball over the net when in fact you were.

Task Sheet

Divided court : Volleyball

Equipment: Defined court area, volleyball net and ball, 3 v 3 or 4 v 4.

```
                            O
        O
                                O
                        X
                                X
            X
```

Task 1:

Each game to be taken to 5 points.
Service to alternate, with players on each team rotating in order.
Winning shots score (whether serving or not).

Serve the ball from anywhere in your court by throwing it over the net into the opposing court. The ball must be caught and thrown, it may not be struck. You may make up to two passes on your side of the net before throwing the ball over into the opposing court.

If you ground the ball in your opponents' court you score a point.

Outcomes:

What strategies have we developed and why?

How do we include all the players in the game?

Example 3 Somerset LEA

Questionnaire to encourage pupil re-flection and to aid the teacher in assessing the pupils' level of under-standing.

Teacher: Paul Stoddart
Class: 1st Year
Activity: Invasion games
Theme: How can we invade the territory?
Teaching style: G. Problem-solving
Questionnaire given after session 2 of a half-term block.

How well have you listened?

1. What ways did your team suggest for involving all team members in the game ?

eg *Not passing to only two people.*
   All our team should have held the ball before shooting at goal.
   Have the not-so-good people attacking.

2. What sort of things could your team do to help it to invade the opponents' goal?

Looking back on the lesson

1. Which way did you think was best to get all of your team-mates involved in your game?

2. Why?

3. What did you do to help your team invade the other team's territory?

eg *I did some dummy runs so that the other team's players would mark me and we would score a goal.*

Example 4 Dudley LEA

Questionnaire to aid pupil self-evaluation.
Teachers: Ian Spode, Julie Dignon, Roy Anderson
Class: 2nd Year
Activity: Basketball Teaching style: C. Reciprocal

Name: *Emma*
Teaching group: *2nd Year*

Section 1

1. Circle around number from 10 (high) to 1 (low):

   I did well as a teacher   10 9 8 ⑦ 6 5 4 3 2 1

   I did well as a performer   10 9 ⑧ 7 6 5 4 3 2 1

   I took an active part in   10 ⑨ 8 7 6 5 4 3 2 1

   all activities

   I enjoyed helping others   10 ⑨ 8 7 6 5 4 3 2 1

   I liked being helped by   10 9 ⑧ 7 6 5 4 3 2 1

   my friends

   I have learned a great   ⑩ 9 8 7 6 5 4 3 2 1
   deal about myself

2. Please rate the following from 1 to 6, with 1 being your
   weakest area and 6 your strongest:

cooperation	*4*
sensitivity to others	*1*
reliability	*6*
consideration for others	*2*
fairness to others	*5*
communication	*3*

8. Was it easier to teach your friends or those you were not
   so friendly with?

   Easier to teach my friends.

9. Did you feel you learned more quickly when being taught
   by your friends?

   Yes, because they understood.

Section 2

1. What part of the course did you enjoy most?
   The teaching.

   Why?   *Because it was exciting.*

2. What part did you enjoy least?
   The ending.

   Why?   *We were just scoring.*

3. What have you learned during this course?
   Quite a lot, like how to jump and shoot properly.

4. Please tick the feelings below which you felt strongly when
   teaching your friends:

   - frustration   ● satisfaction ✓
   - tension   ● failure
   - competitiveness   ● fear ✓
   - success ✓   ● pressure

5. I helped my friends to …
   slow down because she seemed too fast.

6. I found it hard to …
   do some of the jumps.

7. In basketball I am bad at …
   shooting sometimes.

8. In basketball I am good at …
   teaching my friends the jump shot.

9. I need more help in …
   the lay-up shot.

10. I have made progress in …
    learning one of the shots.

11. Do you think you have made a contribution to these
    lessons?
    Yes, because I tried my best.

9. EVALUATION AND CONCLUSION

9.1 Evaluation

The group that worked on producing this booklet discussed what form the overall evaluation of the project should take. But when the report from Norfolk was received, it was unanimously felt that their full and interesting project evaluation summed up the feelings of all those who had participated. It is true that their evaluation refers specifically to one group of teachers and, as it happened, to one style of teaching. But almost all the points included are generally applicable, and were voiced in a similar form by many other teachers.

The Norfolk survey: Problem-solving/Divergent Teaching Style

The involvement of the Norfolk LEA in the National Study Group enabled colleagues to consider more specifically their approach towards the teaching of physical education. As a result of their participation the team members have shared their experiences with colleagues, both within their school and in the department as a whole. It is anticipated that this initiative will promote a comprehensive review of PE teaching within the county.

Initially colleagues voiced certain apprehensions about the national project. The openness and range of approach at national level made them feel vulnerable to criticism from colleagues. However, through much discussion with team members, colleagues in schools, references to national documents and INSET sessions colleagues required confidence to clarify and confirm their own area of study, each responding to a particular need within the department.

During the survey one noticed colleagues assume a greater confidence and sense of purpose in their understanding and in the development of their own projects. They developed an awareness and an appreciation of different teaching strategies and styles, and of their individual and collective contribution to the learning process. Admittedly all members felt vulnerable in this new area of work — a natural reaction to change. But at the same time there was a sense of purpose which gave them the confidence to experiment and share their successes and failures with their colleagues.

Lack of time was a major inhibiting factor in some of the more creative and interdisciplinary approaches that colleagues had intended to include in their project time; and the unsettled and changing environment of the teaching profession did detract from some of the perceived outcomes.

Throughout the survey, team members recorded and monitored their

"As a department it has made us more aware of our teaching style and enabled pupils to participate in the execution of their lesson."

"... first-hand experience of making, creating, inventing something of their own led to self-satisfaction and greater self-confidence. It has also improved group cooperation and social interaction."

"I helped my friends to teach easily by doing everything they told me to."

"I found it hard to teach and watch at the same time."

"It was exciting and it made a change from working by yourself."

work. As a result of individual project evaluation and regular discussion with members, certain observations and concerns emerged:

Areas of Concern

The selected teaching strategy — problem-solving (divergent) — was difficult to apply to lower-ability groups, because of:

- lack of concentration;
- the need for immediate, positive results;
- the traditional concept of the team game.

The pupils' lack of readiness to involve themselves in problem-solving activities was conditioned by:

- inappropriate background experiences (if any) from the primary school;
- pupils not being used to assuming responsibility in learning situations;
- pupil expectations of the role of the PE teacher, based on the traditional model;
- expectations of PE in the secondary school.

The teachers' concern to meet the needs of each pupil tended to lead to:

- over-reaction to change or new ideas in teaching methodology;
- loss of self-confidence for no good reason.

New approaches in teaching strategy and style led to concerns about:

- the use of language in order to present task-solving situations;
- the lack of time to prepare a more complex integrated approach to teaching;
- safety implications where pupils assumed increased responsibility.

Observations on Different Teaching Approaches

The selection of an activity affected teaching strategy in both the long and the short term:

- Some approaches were more easily related to certain games activities.
- Hockey and cricket were thought to present certain difficulties in relation to a comprehensive teaching approach.

The composition of the group affected the success of a selected teaching strategy:

- Different emphases were needed to account for group size, ability, attitude and experience.
- Differentiation was a major factor in determining teaching strategy and style.

Lack of facilities, certain resources or the right conditions affected the continuity and development of a teaching style:

- Progress was restricted by industrial action and weather conditions.
- The selection of teaching strategies was dictated by the lack of indoor facilities and limitations of time and equipment.

Selected teaching styles such as problem-solving (divergent) were more effective in a small-group situation. This affected:

- staffing levels;
- timetabling.

Enjoyment was considered an important factor in learning. In the initial stages of a new approach, time was needed to consider:

- the need to offer immediate reassurance to some pupils, particularly the less able;
- balance in the mental and physical input of each lesson;
- changes to a previously "secure" learning situation.

When employing a new teaching style, there was a need to emphasise:

- simplicity in approach, never assuming too much;
- logical progression;
- sharing the aims and purpose of the lesson with pupils.

Advantages of this New Teaching Approach

It considered the needs of individual pupils far more; therefore there was greater emphasis upon differentiation when preparing lessons.

In all the projects the pupils enjoyed the sharing of ideas and helping each other far more to achieve a common target.

It encouraged long-term planning of PE programmes, assisted in the overall consolidation of the aims and objectives of PE, and demonstrated the general teaching principles that may be successfully applied in all areas of the curriculum.

It encouraged greater professional dialogue and mutual support, leading in particular to increased cross-phase and cross-curricular work, and departmental INSET initiatives.

It has indicated the need for a remedial programme in PE.

Colleagues find the reviewed approach has made pupils more enlightened and enthusiastic in their approach, even in a traditional programme.

It has highlighted the need to appreciate more fully the *process* rather than the *product* of teaching styles and strategies.

> As a result of the Norfolk LEA's participation in the National Study Group, the teachers involved are more aware of the contribution of PE to education as a whole, and in particular of what it is able to offer each pupil.

9.2 Conclusion

> "It is the perceived or subjective newness of the idea for the individual that determines his reaction to it. If the idea seems new to an individual it is an innovation."
>
> [Rogers and Shoemaker 1971]

Throughout this project the emphasis has been on the *process* of teaching in order to enhance pupil learning. The greater the variety of approach used by the teacher, the more likely it is that all pupils will become involved and interested. All teachers should have a variety of teaching styles within their repertoire, incorporating a wide range of strategies; and they should be able to select the appropriate style for the desired outcome.

For some teachers, understanding the strategies and the styles they create, and gaining the ability (and the confidence) to use them, may mean a change in their habitual teaching behaviour. It is important to exercise caution when embarking on a change, and to be clear about the purpose of the change.

To be effective, change must start from where the teacher and the pupil are, and move in small steps. If too great a change is made, particularly over a short period, this is likely to be ineffective and uneconomic, as the benefits will be lost rather than assimilated. It could be even worse than that, because lack of success may lead to loss of confidence by the pupil, the teacher or both. Neither may be willing to try again, so that the final outcome might be an even firmer grip on familiar procedures, especially those where the teacher makes most of the decisions and requires the pupil simply to respond.

To be effective, change must be preceded by careful reflection on the desired outcome in relation to present values and achievements. There must be a clarity of purpose in initiating change. There must also be a firm belief on the part of the teacher in the value of attempting such change.

To be effective, change requires the agreement of all participants, especially in a team situation. Agreement between teachers is particularly important in a departmental structure, where mutual support is essential when attempting change.

Time is needed for change to be effective. Time is needed in order to explore, to reflect, to assimilate and to adapt. If the process is hurried, or too much is expected too soon, the likely outcome will be unsatisfactory, or at best only temporary in its effect.

Yet change is part of progress. Today's children are different from those of a decade ago. Society is continually changing, and we are concerned with educating young people to be able to cope with tomorrow's society. It is essential that all teachers, particularly those involved in physical education, are alive to the potential of a teaching/learning situation. They must be aware of a whole range of teaching strategies and styles, and must be willing to use them effectively to provide real help in the education of the children in their charge.

PART IV

APPENDIX

"I found reciprocal teaching a useful strategy for refining the psycho-motor skills for set tasks which can be reproduced on task cards."

"The project has been interesting and worthwhile, but where are the resources to support further work?"

The best resources are frequently those developed locally by small groups of teachers working together to broaden their range of teaching styles and strategies by discussion, experimentation, team teaching and microteaching.

In addition, many LEAs and most higher-education establishments engaged in training PE teachers have produced (or are currently producing) more general PE resources for local teachers and/or students. The project team sent out a questionnaire to all such institutes and LEAs. The information below has been collated from the results of this survey. It is listed under the following categories:

1. Resources with specific emphasis on teaching styles and strategies.

2. Locally produced written resources on PE in general.

3. Audiovisual resources on PE in general.

A1.1 Resources with Specific Emphasis on Teaching Styles and Strategies

Books

Brandes D & Ginnis P, *A Guide to Student-centred Learning.* Basil Blackwell, 1986.

Brown G, *Microteaching: A Programme of Teaching Skills.* Methuen, 1975.

Hellison D, *Goals and Strategies for Teaching Physical Education.* Human Kinetics, 1984.

Mosston M & Ashworth S, *Teaching Physical Education.* Merrill, 1986 (3rd ed).

Perrott E, *Effective Teaching.* Longman, 1982.

Shipman M, *The Management of Learning in the Classroom.* Hodder and Stoughton, 1985.

Thorpe R, Bunker D & Almond L, *Rethinking Games Teaching.* Loughborough University, 1986.

Waterhouse P, *Managing the Learning Process.* McGraw-Hill, 1983.

Journals

The Bulletin of Physical Education
(BAALPE) (a range of articles).

PEA Journal (a range of articles).

AV Material

Mellor W, *Using Mosston's Spectrum
of Teaching Styles in Basketball*.
1987. A video made during a course
at the College of St Paul and St Mary,
Cheltenham. Available at several
higher-education establishments.

A1.2 Locally Produced Written Resources on PE in General

England and Wales

Berkshire

*Physical Education 5–12 years:
A Developmental Approach.*

*Physical Education: Curriculum
Guidelines.*

Available from:
PE Adviser, Shire Hall, Shirfield Park,
Reading RG2 9KE.

Bury

Curriculum Development Units upon:

1. *Curriculum Leadership in Primary
   School PE.*
2. *Basketball: Introducing the Game.*
3. *Dance in the Primary School.*
4. *The Introduction of Rugby Union
   and Football in Schools.*

Cleveland

See materials in the PE Resources
Centre based in LEA Educational
Development Centres.

Clwyd

*Gymnastics in the Junior School.
PE in the Infant School.*

Available from:
PE Adviser, Shire Hall, Mold, Clwyd.

Coventry

*Coventry Teachers Reflect ... on
Aspects of Student-centred Learning.
Curriculum Development in PE* (a
range of titles).

Available from:
Elm Bank Teachers' Centre, Mile
Lane, Coventry CV1 2LQ.

Devon

*Guidelines for Curriculum Leaders in
Primary Schools.*

*Body Management Skills and Games
in the Primary School.*

PE in Infant Schools.

*Teaching of Swimming in Primary
Schools.*

PE in Bad Weather (for secondary
specialists).

Available from:
Devon Books, Hennock Road, Marsh
Barton, Exeter EX2 8RP.

Hertfordshire

Hertfordshire Primary Series:

*Expressive Movement and Dance.
Games Activities.*

Gymnastics.

*Special Needs: PE in schools for
children with several learning
difficulties.*

Available from:
PE Adviser, Dacorum DEO, Hemel
Hempstead, Herts HP1 1UQ.

Jersey

*The Teaching of Dance in Primary
Schools.*

*The Teaching of Swimming in
Jersey's Schools.*

Kirklees

PE in First and Middle Schools.

Available from PE Adviser.

Northamptonshire

A wide range of LEA guidelines and
booklets.

Available from PE Adviser.

Tyne and Wear

Targets in Primary PE.

Available from:
Centre for Sport, Newcastle University.

Greater London

ILEA 1988

"My Favourite Subject" (The McIntosh
Report): *PE and School Sport.*

Available from ILEA Learning Material
Service:

Lower Primary Gymnastics.

Available from the College of PE:

Junior Gymnastics.

Primary Games.

Providing Equal Opportunities for Girls and Boys in PE.

Enfield

Back to Basic Body Use in PE, by J Handley.

Available from:
Mrs H Mulford, Advisers' Assistant, Education Department, PO Box 56, Civic Centre, Silver Street, Enfield EN1 3XQ.

Harrow

Movement in the First School.

Available from PE Adviser.

Havering

Gymnastics in the Infant School.

Gymnastics in the Junior School.
Available from PE Adviser.

Scotland

Standard grade materials.

Available from:
Bob Brewer, National Development Officer, 7 Dudley Drive, Hyndland, Glasgow G12 9SE.

A1.3 Audio-visual Resources on PE in General

Clwyd PE Advisory Service:

Identifying Movement.
Gymnastic Skills.

Northamptonshire PE Advisory Service:

What did Johnny do today?

Outdoor Education.

ILEA Learning Materials Service:

Lower Primary Gymnastics 1.

Lower Primary Gymnastics 2.

Lower Primary Gymnastics 3.

Lower Primary Gymnastics Notes.

Junior Gymnastics 1.

Junior Gymnastics 2.

Junior Gymnastics 3.

Junior Gymnastics Notes.

Secondary Dance 1.

Secondary Dance 2.

Secondary Dance 3.

Secondary Dance Notes.

Secondary Gymnastics 1.

Secondary Gymnastics 2.

Secondary Gymnastics 3.

Secondary Gymnastics Notes.

Teaching Primary Gymnastics.
Chiltern Consortium, 1977

Health-related Fitness.

College of St Paul and St Mary, Cheltenham.

Many LEAs have prepared audio-visual PE curriculum development resources for local use only.

A2. USEFUL ADDRESSES

Regional/LEA Contacts for Further Information/Support

Most LEA advisory sections, and most higher-education establishments which teach PE, have staff who would be able to offer information and/or support for those wishing to extend and develop their teaching styles and strategies.

In response to a recent BAALPE survey, the following contacts were specifically named:

A2.1 Local Education Authorities

England and Wales

Avon

Mary Harlow
PE Adviser
Avon House North
St James Barton
Bristol
BS99 7EB
Tel: (0272) 290777

Berkshire

Miss E Kershaw
PE Adviser
Shire Hall
Shirfield Park
Reading
RG2 9KE
Tel: (0734) 875444

Bolton

Alan Jeffers
PE Coordinator
Teacher Coordinators'
Centre
Castleton Street
Bolton
BL2 2JW

Clywd

Senior Adviser for PE
Shire Hall
Mold
Clwyd
Tel: (0352) 2121

Coventry

Mrs J Wilson
Curriculum Support Team
Casselden House
Greyfriars
Coventry
Tel: (0203) 831791

East Sussex

Andy Sibson
PE Teacher
Cavendish School
Eldon Road
Eastbourne
East Sussex
BN21 1NE

Gwynedd

PE Adviser
Education Department
Caernarvon
Gwynedd
Tel: (0286) 4121

Hereford and Worcester

Mrs K Van Berlo
Advisory Teacher PE/Dance
County Dance Centre
Spetchley Road
Worcester

Hertfordshire

M Abrahams
PE Advisory Teacher
Dacorum DEO
Hemel Hempstead
HP1 1UQ
Tel: (0442) 60161

Jersey

Alan Cross
PE Adviser
Education Department
PO Box 142
St Saviour
Jersey
Tel: (0534) 71065

Kirklees

J Oxley
PE Adviser
Education Department
Oldgate
Huddersfield
Kirklees

Northamptonshire

Miss A J Perkins
PE Adviser
Education Department
County Hall
Northampton

North Yorkshire

R H Allinson
Senior Adviser
County Hall
Northallerton
North Yorkshire
DL7 8AE
Tel: (0609) 780780

Rotherham

PE Advisers
Education Offices
Norfolk House
Walker Place
Rotherham
S60 1QT
Tel: (0709) 382121

Sheffield

PE Advisers
Education Department
Leopold Street
Sheffield 1

Tyne and Wear

Bernard Jones
Centre for Sport
Newcastle University
Newcastle-upon-Tyne
Tel: 091-232 8511

Walsall

Miss J M Brookes
PE Adviser
Education Department
Civic Centre
Darwall Street
Walsall
Tel: (0922) 650000

Wolverhampton

T Bayliss
PE Inspector
The PE Centre
110 Penn Road
Wolverhampton
WV3 9LH
Tel: (0902) 312160

Greater London

ILEA

Stephen Pain
Centre for PE
16 Paddington Street
London
W1M 4BS
Tel: 01-481 4804

Enfield

S Lloyd
PE Adviser
Education Department
PO Box 56
Civic Centre
Enfield
Middlesex
EN1 3XQ

Harrow

Mrs M Emmans
PE Adviser
PO Box 22
Civic Centre
Harrow
Middlesex
HA1 2UW

Havering

D Baker
PE Adviser
Education Offices
Mercury House
Mercury Gardens
Romford
RM1 3DR
Tel: 01-478 3020

Redbridge

R Makin
PE Adviser
Education Office
255/257 High Road
Ilford
Essex

Scotland

Grampian

Mike Rhodes
PE Adviser
Education Department
Woodhill House
Westburn Road
Aberdeen
AB9 2LU
Tel: (0224) 682222

A2.2 Contacts in Higher Education

Cheshire

Peter Harrison
Crewe + Alsager College of HE
Alsager
Cheshire
ST7 2HL

Gloucestershire

Centre for Curriculum Development
The College of St Paul and St Mary
The Park
Cheltenham
GL50 2RH

Leeds

Malcolm Butterworth and Mervyn Beck
Leeds Polytechnic
Carnegie School of PE and HMS
Beckett Park
Leeds
LS6 3QH

Liverpool

C Jones
University of Liverpool
PO Box 147
Liverpool
L69 3BX

Sheffield

D Crutchley
Principal Lecturer
Sheffield City Polytechnic
Collegiate Crescent Site
Sheffield 10

A3. MEMBERS OF THE NATIONAL STUDY GROUP

| Gwen Cavill | Convenor |
| Jo Coe | Consultant |

Barnet

Stuart Gray	LEA Adviser
S Holland M Peplow K Henderson	Ashmole School
B Wilson	Bishop Douglass School

Dudley

Peter Whitlam	LEA Adviser
Ruth McShane	Ashwood Park Primary School
Julie Dignon	High Park School
Roy Anderson	The Coseley School
Ian Spode	Advisory Teacher

Norfolk

Pauline Penny	LEA Adviser
Chris Price	Dereham Northgate High School
P Tebay	King Edward VII High School, Kings Lynn
Elizabeth Tyler	Downham Market High School

Redbridge

Rita Makin	LEA Adviser
Leslie Hindmarsh	Trinity RC High School
Judith Rock	Mayfield High School

Rotherham

Margaret Griffith	LEA Adviser
Chris Rose	LEA Adviser
Ivy Dorchester Heather Mile R Garnshaw John Gray	Kimberworth Comprehensive School
Mavis Taylor	Thrybergh Comprehensive School
Pat Mitchell C Cox G Brammer	Wath Comprehensive School
R Selkirk	Aston Comprehensive School

Somerset

Gwen Cavill	LEA Adviser
Ann-Marie Latham	Crispin School, Street
Paul Stoddart	King Alfred's School, Burnham-on-Sea
Debra Wilcox	St Andrew's Junior School, Burnham-on-Sea

Sunderland

Chris Short	LEA Adviser
J Young	Hylton Red House School
J Sturrock	Biddick School, Washington

Surrey

Sharon Robinson	LEA Adviser
Alison Vinai	Bishop David Brown School
Sylvia Mundy	South Farnham Middle School
Olia Inak	Therfield Secondary School

Walsall

Jackie Brookes	LEA Adviser
D Gott	T P Riley Community School
Jackie Callicott	Alumwell Community School
Sue Orton	Leamore JMI School